The Gingerbread Man

The Gingerbread Man

Pat Williams — Then and Now

by
Pat Williams
and
Jerry B. Jenkins

A. J. HOLMAN COMPANY
Division of J. B. Lippincott Company
Philadelphia & New York

U.S. Library of Congress Cataloging in Publication Data

Williams, Pat, birth date
    The gingerbread man: Pat Williams—then and now.

    1. Williams, Pat, birth date   2.   Conversion.
I. Jenkins, Jerry B., joint author.   II.   Title.
BV4935.W54A33   248′.2′0924 [B]   74–11309
ISBN–0–87981–038–6

To Jill Marie:
more worth the wait than I can say.

P.W.

And to
Dale LeRoy Thompson

J.J.

Contents

An eight-page section of illustrations follows p. 120

Preface

I met Pat Williams in January of 1972 when the Chicago Bulls were at the peak of their awakening in the National Basketball Association. The young general manager was enjoying national publicity.

I found him a nervous, fast-talking, easy-smiling young executive. He was the youngest general manager in the history of professional sports. He wasn't the hotshot gimmick artist I had imagined. Despite his willingness to talk, Williams was shy in a humble sort of way. Sharply dressed and obviously in shape physically, here was a man who thoroughly enjoyed his life.

His office in the Sheraton Chicago was spacious, and an autographed color picture of Billy Graham decorated a shelf. Perhaps it was the picture that made almost every interviewer describe Pat as a Sunday school type. But he *did* look rosy-cheeked, freshly scrubbed, youthful, and all that. It became obvious during our short conversation that there was more to this thirty-two-year-old front office exec than a ten-year story of success. Much more.

Luckily, between our first meeting and the time we started working together on this book Pat married. His beauty-queen wife, Jill, adds another dimension to his story, but most of all, she has kept her husband recording his thoughts on tape. Even after the frequent Hawk losses. And even when the memories seemed dull and Pat was just sure they wouldn't relate to the book.

It has been a genuine pleasure to work with Pat on his story—the story of the most exciting sports promoter since Bill Veeck. Here is the story of Pat Williams, former Gingerbread Man, and jet-setter extraordinaire.

Excellence is doing your best,
trying your hardest,
and never saying,
"That's good enough."

1

Carney Barker in Doubleknit

Hurry! Hurry! Hurry! Ladies and gentlemen, step right up! For just the price of a book, I'm gonna tellya a story. It's a story 'bout me, mostly how I'm different than I used to be. Gather 'round. Stand close! You may see a little of yourself here, folks!

Do you wish for success? Think it'll bring you happiness and satisfaction? Or have you been there and found that it's not all it's cracked up to be? I have. Stick around and I'll *really* tellya a story.

Come with me to the land of professional sports. And to the glamour of the front office. Don't go 'way, ladies! I've got a love story here, too. Besides being Fergie Jenkins's catcher, running a minor league franchise, winning awards, and switching from baseball to basketball six years ago, I got my life changed. I also married a beauty queen! So step right up!

Hurry! Hurry! Hurry!

I've never really been a circus ringmaster, but I've been called that (and more) during my career in the front offices of professional sports teams. I simply believe

13

that a ballgame should be fun for the spectator. He owes the ballclub nothing. When he pays up to ten dollars for a seat, he deserves the best show we can give him.

If that means pie-eating contests, jugglers, wrestling bears, trick hogs, or weight lifters, then that's what we'll give 'im.

Of course, nothing packs in a crowd like a winning ballclub, but I've found that if the fan remembers a good time, win or lose, he'll be back. There were times in the early days of my career with the Chicago Bulls basketball team when I wondered if *anything* would bring the fans to the stadium. We had a great coach and some good ballplayers, but the club was fairly new in the league and had no winning reputation.

One night before a game in 1969 a man came to the ticket booth with his wife and two children. He rapped on the window and woke up Dick Gonski, our sales director. "I'd like four tickets to the game," he said. "When does it start?"

Dick shook his head. "Sir," he said, "for four tickets, when would you like it to start? For four tickets, we'll come over to your place and play!"

My goal in Atlanta, where I'm general manager of the Hawks basketball team, is to fill the house for every home game and to win the National Basketball Association championship as soon as possible. A championship and a full house have been my goals for every team I've been involved with.

In both Chicago and Atlanta I've worked with fiery little coaches whose histories included traditions of winning at the college level. Cotton Fitzsimmons, the Atlanta coach, has found it tough to accept losing almost as many games as he wins (which is the norm for even many good NBA clubs). Last season the team just couldn't seem to get untracked. They'd win a game, then lose three, then win one and lose three more.

Cotton tried everything to psych up the players. One night he centered his pregame pep talk around the word *pretend*. He said, "Guys, I want you to *pretend* that you're the greatest basketball team in the world. And I want you to *pretend* that this game is for the NBA championship. And I want you to *pretend* that instead of a three-game losing streak, we're on a three-game winning streak. Now go get 'em!"

With that, the Hawks raced out on the floor and were trounced by the Boston Celtics. Cotton was shattered. As he trudged off the floor, all-star guard Pete Maravich ran past and slapped him on the back. "Cheer up, coach," he said, "*pretend* we won!"

All NBA coaches have problems with the referees, but don't let anyone tell you that Cotton and the refs don't get along. More than once I've seen him before the game, helping a ref feel his way into the stadium. And at Christmas he sends each one a card ... in Braille.

Seriously, I enjoy working with Cotton. It's hard on him to have a losing season, but I think he'll prove to be one of the most respected coaches in the NBA. He is one of the reasons I enjoy working in Georgia.

Another reason is that I had contact with someone from Griffin, Georgia, before I ever dreamed I'd wind up working here. During the mid-sixties, when I was general manager of the Philadelphia Phillies minor league baseball club in Spartanburg, South Carolina, the First Baptist Church there called its pastor, Rev. Allister C. Walker, from Griffin. The Scottish preacher made a real impression on me and helped challenge me to a personal confrontation with Christ. One of the first opportunities I ever had to share my new faith was from the pulpit of his church.

I was fairly young to be the general manager of a pro team back then, and I'd like to be able to say that I was in the front office because my sparkling playing career had ended with an injury or something. Actually, I began catching professionally when I was twenty-two. I retired at twenty-three. You probably think I was another Yogi Berra or Johnny Bench, made my fortune quick, and moved on to more challenging pursuits. Nope—my early departure from the playing end of baseball was due as much to a .204 batting average as to anything else.

I never really made much money playing anyway. When the Phillies signed me and assigned me to their Class D club in Miami, they gave me a five-hundred-dollar bonus—in installments. The first installment was enough to get me to Miami. The second was enough to get me back. The owner, Bob Carpenter, advised me to keep the financial terms confidential. "Don't worry," I assured him. "I'm just as ashamed of this contract as you are."

I realized quickly that my future did not lie in major league baseball. I can say that I was Fergie Jenkins's first catcher (though he enjoys denying it). He used to tell the reporters in Miami that the toughest guy to pitch to in the Florida State League was Pat Williams, his catcher!

The early scouting reports on me didn't do much for the ego either. The first report back to the parent club read, "This Williams kid isn't big, but he's slow." Later, I was described as "being in the twilight of a mediocre career." Thus, a coat and tie were tossed my way and I switched to the administrative end of things. Two years later I was general manager of the Spartanburg Phillies in the Western Carolinas League. We had some great teams in Spartanburg (as you'll see later), but I've never counted on a winning team to bring in the fans. If every club in the league depended on a championship to draw spectators, only a select few teams would enjoy decent crowds.

In Atlanta I can't promise a Hawk victory every night. I *can* promise that the guys will give 100 percent. And I *can* promise that the greatest athletes in the United States will be playing the country's most popular game. But all I guarantee the fan is that every trip into the Omni,

Atlanta's beautiful basketball stadium, will be fun and entertaining. If I can add a little icing to the cake and provide a few laughs along with the game, then maybe he'll be back.

By the time I got to Chicago in 1969 I had already seen how successful promotional gimmicks could be in Spartanburg and Philadelphia. I tried everything I knew to fill the stadium. Even if I had accomplished my goals of a full house every night and a championship, I'm sure I would have been remembered not for that, but for wrestling a seven-foot, six-hundred-pound bear during halftime of a game in 1970.

I thought it was smart to bill Victor the Wrestling Bear and offer a little prize to any volunteer opponents. Chicago is known as a tough town, but no one in the stands was foolish enough to tangle with that beast. Except me. Well, I had to. The show must go on and all that, right?

I slipped off my jacket and my glasses and made a quick detour to a pay phone. I knew I was in trouble when Dial-A-Prayer hung up on me! As I walked back toward the waiting bear, I prayed, "Lord, if You're for the bear, may his first blow be swift and painless. And, Lord, if You're for me, may this little penknife find its mark. If You're neutral, these people are going to see some kinda bear fight."

I was pinned three times in twenty seconds.

But, hey, I've got better stories than that. Take a peek at my story on the following pages and see what it's like to run a pro basketball team. I'll be reminiscing about growing up in Wilmington, Delaware; playing baseball at Wake Forest and then for the Phillies; the flat, stale taste of success in Spartanburg; getting into the NBA in Philadelphia; experiencing highs and lows in Chicago; and finally moving to Atlanta, the land of Maravich, Hudson, Bellamy. . . .

Hurry! Hurry! Hurry! Step right up and move in close!

2

Popsicle

At my mother's home in Wilmington, Delaware, there are still two stones about sixty feet apart in the yard. One is about the size of home plate, the other the size of a pitcher's slab. My father, Jim Williams, had given me a catcher's glove when I was three years old, a few years before I would even be able to handle it. But after he took me to a big league game at Shibe Park in Philadelphia when I was seven, I was hooked. The old Athletics played the Cleveland Indians that day. I remember that we sat through both games, and that Bob Feller did not pitch in either. And my older sister, Carol, and I bothered Dad all afternoon for pop and hotdogs. But I don't remember precisely what it was that impressed me so dramatically. All I know is that when I awoke the next morning, I no longer wanted to be a farmer or a naturalist or a policeman. I knew I was going to be a big league baseball player. For more than fifteen years, I never doubted it.

I lived baseball. I always had my mitt with me, and I'd throw a spare glove to anyone walking by. Play catch? Hit a few? Even Mom got into the act. She was quite a baseball fan. One day, when I was pitching to her and she was batting balls back to me, she misjudged her swing and nailed me with a line drive. Right in the eye. I went down like a sack of potatoes and Mom was scared to death. I hardly knew what had hit me. We laugh about it now, but she thought she'd killed me.

I tell her that I should have jumped right up and thrown a brushback pitch at her. Early Wynn brushed back so many batters in his big league career that people say he would have thrown at his own mother. "I would if she was crowdin' the plate," he'd always say.

I didn't care much for reading and arithmetic, and I don't know how literate I'd be today if it hadn't been for the sports pages of *The New York Times*. After that first doubleheader in Philadelphia, I checked the box scores every day. Checking the averages and studying the won-lost columns helped me learn to read and figure. The backs of baseball cards helped too. I became a bubble gum freak and made Mother drive me all over Wilmington to find stores that sold the nickel packs.

It seems I always had a bat in my hands. I put tape on the full-length mirror in my room to mark off my strike zone, and I'd swing the bat for hours. Once I cracked our dog in the head! (I wasn't a bad kid, but Dad kept a big paint paddle in the kitchen. He called it his "Patrick Persuader.")

Mostly I played ball with Dad. He was thin and wiry. And without temper. Mom made up for that. They were quite different. Both had their own interests and concerns, and, while they were close, they really went their separate ways during the day. Our family was like that. Besides Carol, I had two younger sisters—Ruthie, three years younger, and Mary Ellen, who was born when I was seven. I cried bitter tears when I learned the new baby was a girl. I wanted a brother so badly. Mary Ellen is mentally retarded and has been institutionalized for nearly thirty years. That was one thing that brought my parents closer together. When they saw the state of research and treatment of retardation in Delaware, they threw themselves into fundraising efforts. Both had been civic-minded and busy, but now they had a single cause.

Our family never took a vacation together. It wasn't that we wouldn't have liked to; we just never got our schedules coordinated. My sisters were good students (both wound up going to Vassar as Mother had), while baseball ruled my life. And I mean *ruled*—every waking moment, as they say.

The wall in my room was literally covered with baseball pictures. I liked all sports, but baseball was to be my career. I knew all the statistics, and I was a nut, as I still am, on baseball memorabilia. When I reflect on that part of my life, all I see in my mind's eye is baseball.

I read somewhere that Rogers Hornsby, the great National League hitting star, never went to the movies. He said he wanted to protect his eyes. If it was good enough for Hornsby, it was good enough for Kid Williams. All through high school, I never went to a movie. (I didn't hit much better, and I missed a lot of good shows.)

I also read that Don Mueller of the New York Giants sharpened his eye for hitting a curve ball by trying to hit corncobs with a broomstick. Every night after that I had my dad firing corncobs at me in the backyard. I'm sure he must have felt ridiculous.

I did everything I could think of to heighten my chances of becoming a big leaguer. I didn't smoke or drink or carouse. We were members of the local Presbyterian Church, so I probably wouldn't have gotten into too many bad habits anyway. I didn't like church much though. I memorized a lot of Bible verses in Sunday school, but during most of the sermons my mind was far away. I would be throwing touchdowns for the Philadelphia Eagles or hitting a homer to win the World Series for the Phillies.

For eighteen years my father taught at Tower Hill School, a private, all-grade school for elite students whose parents could afford it. I'd like to think I'd have gone there anyway, but I went because of him. He made very little money as a teacher and coach, but teachers' kids went free. It was great to have a coach for a father. We never hassled each other. I remember that I always knew I could go to him with anything, though I seldom did. Today I wish that I had.

When I was in the sixth grade in 1952, Dad quit at Tower Hill to go into the insurance business. I cried and cried that day. I suppose I thought I'd miss the glamour of being the son of the varsity coach, but I know now that it was probably the best thing that could have happened. It was necessary financially for Dad to find other work. And I probably would have felt uncomfortable playing for my own father anyway.

Dad was an immediate and consistent success in life insurance—he was so friendly and outgoing that he could hardly have missed. He was enthusiastic about me and my interests to the point that he embarrassed me, shooting pictures, taking movies, hollering, and talking to everyone at my ballgames. I'll probably be much the same kind of father, but more than once I gave him directions to the wrong ballpark. He always found me, and I don't know if he ever realized I had done it intentionally. I hope not. He just loved me. And he cared. I wonder sometimes how I could have lived in the same house with the man for eighteen years without having taken the time to get to know him better.

My Uncle Bill Parsons was always involved, too. He took my friends and me to Philadelphia to see major league games and played catch with us many weekends. He was a coach at the Haverford School just outside Philly. Uncle Bill still shows interest in me and my career.

I developed into a good baseball player and football quarterback and was fair at basketball. It's ironic that I wound up in the one sport I excelled in least. Back then, even football took a backseat to baseball for me. I hung around with the other Tower Hill athletes in the neighborhood. My best friend was Ruly Carpenter, son of the owner of the Philadelphia Phillies.

Mike Castle and Reeves Montague ran with us too.

None of us were very social minded—no dating. We went to basketball games every weekend, and we played whatever sports were in season. With Dad having been a teacher and Mother and the girls having good academic backgrounds, I was really a stranger at home. I guess it's kind of boorish to have a sports nut and a mediocre student in a family like that. But I was oblivious. Outside my group of guys, I was shy. All I cared about was sports.

Mike and Reeves and I always vowed that we would never be lovers. I broke the vow in eighth grade after taking an hour to work up enough courage to dial Patsy Cox's number. She was the cutest girl at Wilmington Friends School, our fiercest rival. I knew I'd hear from Mike and Reeves and all the guys who thought dating someone from a rival school was some sort of sin, but Patsy was really something.

The evening was embarrassing, it being a first for me. I bluffed my way through a Tower Hill School dance and tried my best to be suave and cool. Polite conversation was difficult for me, but I had to grin and bear it as Patsy sat between me and my dad in the front seat of the family car to and from the school. After I walked Patsy to her door and stood there scuffing my shoes on the sidewalk for five minutes, I jumped back in the car with great relief. Then who should appear from the floor of the backseat but Carol, my older sister. Grief! She and Dad had a good laugh. I fumed, and it was four years before I worked up enough courage to ask anyone else out.

Ruly Carpenter was a great athlete and wound up starring in football and baseball at Yale. His father still owns the Philadelphia Phillies, and Ruly is now their president. You'd never have guessed Ruly was from such a wealthy family. He was as plain as an old shoe and always in the middle of mischief.

Mom and Dad were leery of my being with Ruly constantly. He was always throwing snowballs or shooting someone's dog or cat with a slingshot. He never really got into serious trouble, but he was something else. At the Carpenters' summer home in southern Delaware during the vacation before our senior year in high school, Ruly and I were floating on rubber rafts in the Atlantic Ocean. We got too far from shore and the lifeguard blew his whistle and waved us back. I was scared and stopped right away, but Ruly was headed for England. He pretended he didn't hear and fearlessly kept paddling. If the police hadn't come out in a boat to get him, he'd still be paddling! My parents didn't enjoy hearing that story.

The good times with Ruly made the frightening ones worth the hassle. Most kids would give their eyeteeth to have been the friend of a major league owner. Often we'd go right into the clubhouse at the ballpark. I met all my Philly idols. In high school, during spring vacation, I even went with Ruly to Clearwater, Florida, where the Phillies held spring training.

By that time we were star athletes at Tower Hill. He was a pitcher, and I was his catcher. It was fun to watch the big leaguers play, but one day he got pretty cocky. We had watched the Phils play at Al Lopez Field in Tampa. Their three weakest hitters, Joe Lonnett, Roy Smalley, and Woody Smith, combined for no hits in twelve times at bat in the game. That night at dinner, Ruly needled his father mercilessly. "Dad, even I could get those bums out."

Ruly had gone too far. Bob Carpenter stood. "Awright, Ruly, you're on," he said. He invented a special game so Ruly could face just Lonnett, Smalley, and Smith. Ruly would pitch and I was to catch. We could choose any of the Phillies to play the infield and outfield for us. Mr. Carpenter bet Ruly twenty dollars that in three innings, Lonnett, Smalley, and Smith would score at least four runs.

What an experience! We weren't going to hit. We just had to get these three guys out nine times before they scored four runs. There I was behind the plate with Ruly on the mound just like at Tower Hill. But the fielders were hardly our high school teammates, and we even had big league umpires.

Ruly won the bet. Joe Lonnett hit a homerun with Smith on base, but those were the only two runs they scored. Ruly even struck out Smalley once. Roy tossed his bat aside and trudged away muttering, "What a way to leave the big leagues." The Philadelphia sportswriters watched the whole fiasco and wrote columns about it. It was really a thrill, easily the highlight of my high school years.

By this time Ruly was past the age where he shot out street lights with his BB gun. He was sought by major colleges for his football and baseball talent. He played end for the football team and I threw him ten touchdown passes our senior year. We were undefeated and enjoyed the unique excitement that goes with a championship team.

We had a good basketball team too, but the baseball season, as always for me, was the highlight. Ruly pitched three no-hitters, and my batting average was over .500. That May I was worried about the game against our rivals from Friends School, not to mention my senior term paper. At breakfast the morning of the game my dad teased me. "Go four-for-four today and I'll type your term paper this weekend," he said.

"Are you serious?" I asked.

"Sure!" He laughed. I can still see him laboring over the typewriter, banging out "Islam as a Force in Africa." I had hit three singles and a double in four times up. (I don't remember when I've been so motivated!)

All of my friends went north to college, most of them to the Ivy League schools. Outside the group, I was still very shy. I didn't want to go to a huge school; I wanted a college with a good baseball program and physical education department. All athletes major in physical education, right? So they can coach when the glorious career is over? I chose Wake Forest in Winston-Salem, North Carolina.

I was scared and homesick for quite a while. Alone. I really had to work hard just to get by academically. Baseball and schoolwork became my life. Dad was still cheerleading. He'd drive the eight- or nine-hour stretch, sometimes all night, from home to Wake Forest to watch me play a freshman game; then he'd travel to wherever the varsity team was playing. Of course, I wasn't even at the varsity games. But he'd go to get involved with my school.

One weekend the varsity was playing at the University of Maryland. Sure enough, Dad drove over to watch the game. He bought ice cream from a Good Humor man and took it into the dugout—one for everyone. Good ol' Dad. I really heard about that one when the varsity returned. They nicknamed me "Popsicle" and that stuck for a while. Dad even embarrassed me when I wasn't around.

He sure watched a lot of baseball. I wish now that he could have seen me play minor league ball. But back then I wouldn't have cared if he'd missed a lot of games.

I started coming out of my shell a bit during the summer after my freshman year. I played semipro ball in Nova Scotia. It was too fast a league for me, but I did stick it out. It was good for me to be that far away from home and school.

My shell was completely broken during the fall of my junior year. I had been doing well in baseball and was getting along gradewise, but for some reason I came in to my own socially that fall. I had always listened intently to radio sports announcers and had a secret longing to broadcast a game. One day I just walked over to the campus radio station WFDD, with the idea of broadcasting the freshman basketball games and doing a sports show. The staff liked the idea. I was forced to articulate to thousands of people from behind a microphone. It was too late to be shy.

I loved it and continued to broadcast sporting events for the next several years whenever I got the chance. I became better known on campus and found it much easier to talk to people. A speech course I took that year and the next under a professor named James Walton really helped too. I still use techniques I learned from him.

A real turning point came in November of that junior year, 1960. Jerry Steele, president of the Monogram Club (the varsity letter winners), needed someone to head up the homecoming activities. The club was to sponsor a basketball game. "Pat, I'm volunteering you," he said.

"Hey, I'd really like to, but I'm so busy. I——"

Jerry was six-foot-eight and weighed 235. He wouldn't let up, so I volunteered. I enlisted the help of other club members and worked my head off to make the thing go. I had the tickets printed and sold and directed the publicity campaign and made arrangements for a halftime show and a band and the homecoming queen presentation and everything. I was merchandising, packaging, and selling basketball as fun and entertainment.

The night after the game I was so excited I could hardly sleep. I knew then that someday I would like to get in on the promotional end of professional sports. But my baseball career came first: there was still this matter of making the big leagues.

I had a great spring. I hit over .300 as the varsity catcher and in a game at Georgia Southern I had four hits in five at bats, including a homerun. Just one more year, and big league baseball, here I come!

The following fall my sports announcing job took me all over the place to interview celebrities. I even interviewed Billy Graham when he visited to speak at chapel. Since Wake Forest was a Baptist college, we had required chapel twice a week. Except for when Dr. Graham was there, all I remember about chapel was that everyone just sat there reading their newspapers. It impressed me that Dr. Graham would speak at Wake Forest, but I was more impressed when big leaguers Roger Maris, Jim Gentile, and Harmon Killebrew visited the campus. They were in Winston-Salem for a homerun-hitting contest. Maris had just finished the 1961 season, during which he had established the season record of sixty-one homeruns. Interviewing him was almost like being in the majors already. I wanted it so badly I could taste it.

The Philadelphia Phillies' area scout, Wes Livengood, was watching my progress and sent reports back to the front office regularly. I had gotten to know him fairly well. We talked a lot, but not much about front office work. I guess he saw something in me that he thought would fit into the administration end of things. I learned later that his reports often dealt more with my front-office potential than my baseball ability. But I didn't know that then. During the spring of 1962 I was a senior on a winning baseball team.

The Yale baseball team came through on a Southern tour, so I got a chance to play a ballgame *against* Ruly for once. I didn't get a chance to bat against him though. He played left field and got one hit, but we won.

We played well enough in our league to tie Virginia for the Atlantic Coast Conference championship. We beat them in the playoff game and won the right to represent the conference in the National Collegiate Athletic Association regional tournament. The first round was in Gastonia. It was a double elimination tournament. Until you lose twice, you're still in. A weekend of competition left Florida State with one loss and Wake Forest undefeated. We would play them in a doubleheader. All we had to do was beat them once, which would give them two losses, and we'd be on our way to Omaha for the NCAA College World Series. Just one game. The pressure was on them.

Back in Winston-Salem our classmates were graduating. Getting to the NCAA playoffs would be worth missing the ceremonies. We just had to win.

We lost the first game badly. Now both teams had lost once. My roommate, Don Roth, would pitch the second game. Winning would catapult us into the College World Series.

3

Shirt Off, Shorts On, Leg Off

Don Roth was pitching a beautiful game for us. The score was tied when I came to bat in the top of the eighth inning with no one on base. I drove a homerun over the left field fence and almost danced around the bases, I was so happy. We were up by one. If we could just hold them for two more innings. . . .

In the bottom of the eighth Florida State scored when a throw to the plate bounced and hit me in the face. I wasn't hurt, but I was determined that they wouldn't score again. I stayed in and kept signaling for Don's wicked curve ball. He struck out six straight hitters with it before a runner reached second in the bottom of the twelfth inning.

The next hitter lined a single into left. I can still remember straddling the plate and reaching for that throw. It seemed to be floating in. The runner had rounded third base and was churning down the line toward me, kicking mud high behind him. I waited and waited and waited. He beat the throw. We had lost.

It hit me all at once. There would be no more ball-games with these guys. And no more Wake Forest. The school year had ended, the class had graduated, the team had lost, it was over. I didn't want to see anyone; I could hardly talk. It was a deep, aching, empty feeling. And here comes Dad. *Doesn't he know I don't want to talk now?*

He tried briefly to console me. I wasn't really listening. Then he said something about his plans to drop Carol off in Washington, D.C., on the way back to Wilmington ... Mother and Ruthie would be taking the other car ... they'd see me at home later. "Yeah, O.K.," I said, hardly paying attention. "Listen, Dad, could you check with Mr. Carpenter and see what my chances are with the Phillies organization?"

"Oh, I think we should wait until you get home, Pat," he said. I trudged toward the team bus for the last ride back to Winston-Salem. We would rather have been whooping and hollering, but under the circumstances the silence was welcome. It was raining hard now. And that was fine with me.

Four friends who lived north of Wilmington traveled with me the next morning. We had slept in late and then took our time packing up our cars before heading north. It was a melancholy time. We didn't talk much. I wanted to shake off the past and think about breaking into pro ball, but the loss was too fresh. Just one day before we had been making plans for a trip to Omaha. Now we were headed home. It hurt. We didn't joke around much—you don't get two shots at the NCAA's. I've suffered a lot of losses since then, but none have bitten so deeply or disappointed me so much as that one.

We didn't push it on the freeway. We stopped frequently for snacks and had a leisurely dinner Tuesday evening. Later we noticed the lights of a minor league ballpark in Richmond, Virginia. We stopped and watched the ballgame. We were in no hurry to leave four years behind.

I had no idea that Mother was trying frantically to get in touch with me. She didn't know exactly when I planned to get home, nor did she know the exact route. All she could do was wait. We stayed overnight in Richmond and slept in again Wednesday morning. The guys accepted my invitation to spend a night at our place in Wilmington. Mother was still waiting. We arrived at about five o'clock Wednesday afternoon.

As we pulled into the drive, I noticed several other cars parked at the curb. Before I could open my door, Mother had run from the house to meet me. She was relieved just to know where I was. She took me aside and we walked to the side of the house. It was obvious something was wrong. If we had been listening to the radio, I'd have already known.

"What is it, Mom?"

"Daddy's had an accident. On the way home after he dropped Carol off." She was crying.

"How bad?" I asked.

"Bad. He was killed."

It had happened after midnight Monday, even before I had left Wake Forest. For some reason we hadn't been listening to the radio. I was numb. Why hadn't I talked to him more after the game? My first thought was for my buddies. It was an embarrassing situation for them; obviously they couldn't stay. I didn't want to break down. I had to play it tough, especially with the guys there. And with all I had to do. The guys begged off quickly and left. I was suddenly in the middle of funeral arrangements, greeting friends and relatives, being the man of the family.

Mother misunderstood my lack of outward emotion. I finally did break down at the funeral. But as soon as the service ended, I felt I had to stand at the door and thank everyone for coming. I'm glad I did.

Suddenly that was over too. I was still left with the question of what I was to do. My mother could have easily shamed me into staying in Wilmington and not leaving her at a time like that. I had been accepted for graduate study at Indiana in the fall, but the most pressing thing to me right then, as always, was pro baseball. I went to see Ruly's dad.

Mr. Carpenter had been at the funeral. He had known my father well, and the combination of my friendship with Ruly and my father's funeral the day before put me in an enviable position before the kindhearted owner of the Phillies. I was not consciously playing on his sympathy. I probably was not good enough to have been signed by a pro club, but I had worked toward this my whole life. Standard procedure calls for the ball team to seek out players. I reversed it. If they had an opening, I wanted it.

"I know Mr. Livengood's reports have been sent in," I said. "I was just wondering what the thinking is." He told me he'd check and call me. The next morning, my lifelong dream came true.

"We've got a spot for you," Mr. Carpenter said. "We need a catcher in Miami." It was their Class D club in the Florida State League. "How are you fixed for cash? Are you broke? We'll give you five hundred dollars to sign and you'll get four hundred a month. Come up to Philadelphia tomorrow and we'll have the contract waiting for you."

A week to the day after the last Wake Forest game, I was on my way to Miami. My head was still spinning from all that had happened. The only thing I knew about Miami was that it was the home of the Fontainebleau Hotel. Ultra-swank. I pulled in there at about midnight and decided that was where I wanted to stay. No vacancies. I had a piece of pie at their coffee shop and went elsewhere.

The last thing Bob Carpenter had said to me before I left was, "Keep your eyes and ears open on the field and off." I think he had Wes Livengood's scouting reports in mind. He didn't expect me to hit .292 that season. Management must have been more surprised than pleased.

We had quite a team down there. Fergie Jenkins was one of the pitchers. I caught five of his seven victories that season. He didn't *really* say I was the toughest guy in the league to pitch to, but that line has sure helped me on the banquet circuit.

Alex Johnson, who led the American League in hitting a few years ago, was just a kid outfielder in Miami in 1962. It was apparent that he was a natural hitter. He liked to razz me all the time. One day while I was taking batting practice he stood outside the cage, baiting me. "Williams," he said, "I hit 'em when I want to. You hit 'em when you can." He led the league in hitting that year.

I found myself spending a lot of time with General Manager Bill Durney. It's unheard of for a player to spend much time with front-office personnel, but he had been Bill Veeck's traveling secretary when Veeck ran the St. Louis Browns in the early 1950s. I had always been fascinated by the promotional genius of Veeck, and I found Durney interesting. What a wealth of experience! I stayed close. For all the years I had been longing for a baseball career, I was certainly finding the front office intriguing.

My eyes were opened to the racial situation in the South that season too. The black ballplayers on our club could not stay at many of the motels we stayed at, nor could they eat at the same restaurants. Often we brought food out to the blacks who had to wait for us on the bus. It absolutely shocked me. I could not understand it then, and I don't understand it today. I never heard one of them complain, though. Of course, this was before blacks were even called blacks. They were "Negroes," and they had not made themselves heard nationally yet.

One of the veteran black players was Fred Mason. He was from my hometown. After we lost to Fort Lauderdale in the playoffs that year, Fred and I took off for

Wilmington. We drove from Miami to Jacksonville where I thought we'd get gas and find a place to spend the night.

I told the attendant to fill it up, then I went into the station for a bottle of pop. After a few minutes, Fred got out of the car and headed toward the rest room. Suddenly the attendant appeared with a huge monkey wrench. "Get outta here, you black nigger!" he hissed. "I'll kill you!" I froze. Fred calmly turned on his heel and walked back to sit in the car as the man cursed him.

I shook as I paid for the gas. We drove straight through to Wilmington, taking turns sleeping and driving. It was over a thousand miles. We were silent for hours before Fred spoke quietly. "Some of my friends would've torn that place apart," he said. "I'm just not that way." That night it would have served the station owner right.

I was pleased with the year I'd had. I wished Dad could have seen some games. He'd have driven all the way to Miami. Somehow I missed even his excited shouting and carrying on. But it was a marvelous summer. I had gotten a real taste of professional baseball, and I had seen a lot of minor league parks. Bill Durney told me that I should look up Bill Veeck sometime. Veeck had moved into a new place in Easton, Maryland, which wasn't far from Wilmington, so I called him one day. I mentioned Durney's name and asked him if I could visit before I left for graduate school at Indiana.

Veeck was very cordial and invited me to his home for a day. I was excited. I hadn't told him that I had any aspirations toward sports promotion, but, when I became very honest with myself, I knew. There was no sense trying to kid anyone. I was not going to make the major leagues as a player. It would take more than a .292 average in the low minors.

I drove down a long, winding, tree-lined driveway and halfway around a circle that led to his house on the

Chesapeake Bay. It was a beautiful fall day. There on the front steps sat Veeck. Burr-headed, bare-chested, one-legged, he wore a pair of tan shorts and was reading a book of Civil War poetry. His own book, *Veeck as in Wreck*, had been out only a few months and had already become a sensational best-seller. (I still read it once a year.)

I expected Veeck to be a loud, brash, Leo Durocher type. I was shocked to find him a warm and sincere man, soft-spoken. He was a great listener and seemed interested in everything I had to say. His brilliant mind is always racing, and his conversation is highlighted by thoughts and a vocabulary amassed through extensive reading.

I'd been there about an hour just chatting, when I began to feel that I was intruding. It was time for lunch. I started to plan a graceful exit when he said, "If Bill Durney finds out I had you here and didn't invite you for lunch, he'll really be mad." We chatted on into the afternoon. He was down-to-earth and friendly. He strapped on his leg and played badminton; he even raced bicycles with his kids that day.

Before I left, he offered four pieces of advice. "First," he said, "know somebody. It's almost impossible to get inside this game if you don't know somebody." I told him of my relationship with the Carpenters. "Good," he said. "Three more things: Learn to type. Learn all you can about advertising and marketing. And get some kind of business background." I memorized the typewriter keyboard on my way to graduate school in Bloomington, Indiana, the next week. For the next eight years I did most of my own typing. I picked up advertising and business through reading and on-the-job training. I can see how well founded Veeck's advice really was. Bill is still a close friend and remains one of the most fascinating personalities I've ever met.

I had chosen Indiana University because of its physical education department and its radio station. I hoped that I could stay involved in sportscasting. Things worked out perfectly. I worked with a guy named John Gutowsky announcing football and basketball on the campus station, WFIU. We became fast friends and spent hours working together.

I stayed at Indiana for two semesters to get as many of my Master's requirements out of the way as I could. The Phils had sent me a new contract which included a fifty-dollar-a-month raise, but by the spring of 1963 I had pretty well leveled with myself about my baseball future. I hadn't told anyone yet, but if I was still banking on making the majors, I never would have skipped spring training to stay in school. The result was that, by the time I joined the team in Miami, the regular season was under way and I was hopelessly out of shape.

I was thrown into the lineup right away. I didn't give myself enough time and quickly acquired a sore arm. The second night I was there I caught a doubleheader against Daytona Beach. I won the first game with a single to drive in the winning run. In the second game my squeeze bunt in the last inning brought in the winning run. From there it was all downhill.

It was not a good summer for me. I didn't feel good and I couldn't get untracked. There's simply no shortcut to getting in shape. I wasn't doing the job. In July, Clay Dennis, the Phillies minor league director, visited Miami. I knew it was time to make my move. My motivation was gone.

Once again I reversed the traditional roles. Rather than letting the Phillies cut me at the end of the season, I went to Clay and resigned. "I'm not contributing," I told him. "I'd be interested, if you'd let me, in spending the last month of the season helping out in the front office. I'm not earning my pay on the field, so I'd be happy to just help Bill Durney any way I can in the office."

Mr. Dennis okayed it, so for the last five weeks or so of the 1963 season I did everything from typing news releases and selling tickets to sorting paper clips and rubber bands. I still caught batting practice and warmed up pitchers, but I made no more road trips and didn't suit up for any games. I was close enough to the team so that the final cutting of the cord, the actual break from my life-long ambition, was not as painful as it might have been. I had known for some time that I wasn't major league material, but it was still hard to admit to everyone else.

Bill Durney really took me under his wing. He was very fatherly, always encouraging and advising me. He was a giant, rotund man and I thoroughly enjoyed working with him. When I left for Indiana for one more semester of graduate work, I looked forward to working with John Gutowsky on the broadcasts again. And I looked forward to getting my Master's in physical education. But something was missing. I no longer knew exactly where I was headed. Before, I had known where every step should lead. At the end of every school year, baseball awaited me. Would I teach, coach, broadcast, or administrate? I didn't know. It was a strange, exciting feeling.

In November I heard from Clay Dennis. We met at Chicago's O'Hare Inn, where he told me that Bill Durney wanted me back. "We want you to spend the 1964 season as assistant general manager of the Miami club," he said. I was speechless. Clay continued. "The pay will be the same as last year. At the end of the season we'll decide where to go from there. If we like it and you like it, who knows?"

When the basketball broadcasting schedule was over, I took my Master's degree and drove to Miami. Bill put me to work right away. He was a fun, hard-working, hard-driving man who lived life to the fullest and never worried about slowing down. He ate relentlessly and seldom slept. My first task was to sell the advertising in the season program. March was fast approaching, so we had to get rolling. The team would arrive soon.

I was terrified. I had never sold anything in my life.

4

Mister R. E. and Sam

All I had to do was sell advertising space in the Miami Marlins' program. It should have been easy, but my approach was all wrong. I'm sure I went around saying things like, "We've got these ads. You wouldn't wanna buy one, would ya?" For two and a half days I was a complete flop. I hadn't sold even a portion of a page—and these were relatively cheap pages. I was just sick about it. I kept trying, but no one even came close to buying.

Finally I bit my lip and went back to Bill Durney's office. It was about noon of my third day out. "I just can't do it, Bill," I said. I realized how badly I wanted to succeed when I couldn't hold back the tears. I was humiliated. I looked down at the sample program rolled up in my hands.

Bill talked slowly and softly. Basically, he simply assured me of his confidence in me and reminded me that I wasn't simply asking for money. I was selling a service, a bargain. I was doing the merchant a favor. For just a few dollars he could put the name of his establishment before the sports public at every ballgame. Bill was selling and I was buying. "Selling is the key to success in this business, Pat. Whether it's your outfield walls, tickets, or

the program, selling is the name of the game." Bill had
an ability to phrase things just so. I took just pages of notes
on the hints he gave. He wanted me to exude confidence
and charisma, the direct opposite of the picture I had presented those first few days out.

I went to Mugge's Restaurant. It was a snap. I had a
bargain. I was doing Mr. Mugge a favor. Why, he'd appre-
ciate my bringing this terrific advertising tool to his attention. When I believed it, the merchants believed it. Mr.
Mugge bought a seventy-five-dollar ad, and after that it
was easy. I sold out the rest of the space in a matter of
days and was ready for my next assignment. I was beginning to like this business.

Bill gave me lots of freedom. We bounced promotional
ideas off each other every day. He was never at a loss for
a gimmick. If it wasn't a crazy contest, it was a high school
band or a giveaway. He always insisted on giving a
prospective advertising client a choice. "Where would you
like your ad," he'd ask, grinning, "next to the Marlin lineup,
or next to the visitors'?" He never mentioned the possibility that the customer might not want his ad in our season
program at all.

Watching this whirlwind at work had a profound
effect on my career. Bill died of a heart attack in 1968.
Many times in later years I'd wonder, *What would Bill
Durney think of this?*

The major league Phillies were in the thick of the
National League pennant race that fall of 1964. Since the
minor league season ends earlier than the majors they
asked me to come to Philadelphia to help with promotion
and ticket sales in the event they played in the World
Series. By that time I was so psyched up about a career
in pro sports administration that I would have done anything to help them out. Anything except to go AWOL. I
had a four-month army obligation to serve, beginning in
September. As it turned out, the Phillies blew the 1964

pennant drive or it would have been even tougher for me to accept.

I had been out on my own for several years and had gotten a taste of the world, so it was humiliating to spend sixteen weeks being treated like a number. For the first few weeks of basic training at Fort Jackson in Columbia, South Carolina, I was treated more like an animal. No phone calls, no leaves, no mail, no nothing. But when I got feeling really low, I considered the alternative—Vietnam. Fort Jackson became a playground.

After basic training I was moved to Fort Polk in Louisiana where the physical grind let up a bit; but it was still a tough experience. The mental pressure was almost unbearable, and I was thrilled when Christmas leave came. The Phillies had asked me to visit them in Philadelphia to discuss the future.

"There are two jobs open," Clay Dennis told me. "Either is yours if you're interested. Pay is five hundred a month." Both were low minor league clubs who needed general managers. One was in Bakersfield, California, and the other was in Spartanburg, South Carolina. You talk about a break! I wasn't twenty-five years old yet and I was being given my choice of general managerships.

I chose the Spartanburg job because of my familiarity with South Carolina. Dick Smith, a former $100,000 bonus baby pitcher in the Phils organization, took the Bakersfield club. He had learned the ropes as assistant G.M. at Little Rock, Arkansas. His high-priced left arm had gone bad, but he was a sharp guy who was valuable to the organization. Dick was a close friend, and almost a decade later he would stand up at my wedding.

My active duty commitment kept me busy until the end of January. I couldn't get out of there fast enough. Here was my first real chance to run the show. I flew to Miami for a couple of days of heavy briefing with Bill Durney, then flew home to spend a couple of days in

Wilmington. I drove back down to Spartanburg; for all my familiarity with the state, I had never been in this city, and I knew no one. I was to look up Mr. R. E. Littlejohn, one of the two owners of the Spartanburg Phillies. It was cold and rainy when I arrived that first Sunday in February 1965. Though the day was miserable, I could feel the excitement right down to my toes.

Mr. Littlejohn is a successful petroleum carrier executive, and his home is huge and beautiful. Mrs. Littlejohn answered my knock. "We were expecting you," she said. "Mister R.E. was called out of town unexpectedly, but please come in." It seems everyone in Spartanburg called her husband "Mister R.E." I did too, at first. Later I began calling him "Coach." Mrs. Littlejohn insisted that I call *her* "Sam." So the two who were to become my closest friends in Spartanburg were Coach and Sam!

Sam and I had a strange conversation that first day. "You'll never meet another man like Mister R.E.," she said. "You'll never again work for anyone like him. He's the greatest man in the world." It's not every day you hear a woman talk about her husband that way, especially a woman in her fifties.

But she was right. Two days later, after I had found a place to stay and had settled in, I met Mister R.E. at his office. I was immediately impressed by this white-haired Southern gentleman. He was a very courteous, soft-spoken man who seemed to enjoy putting people at ease. No one was intimidated in his presence. He was the type of man whose demeanor would convince you he didn't see you fall in the mud, even if it happened right in front of him.

He was unlike any businessman I had ever met. He seemed to love everyone he dealt with. Never sarcastic or pushy, he was different and that intrigued me. I couldn't put my finger on what made him stand out so, and I hardly had time to worry about it. The season would open in just two months.

The ballfield, Duncan Park, was unbelievable. It was set low in a hilly, tree-filled area. The location was beautiful, but the stadium itself was run-down, dirty, unpainted. The office was tiny and cold, and the rest rooms were an abomination. I was overwhelmed with a sense of helplessness. Here was my big chance; I was going to be an executive. But who was going to fix up this ballpark?

Not only was I the boss, but I was also the staff. Mister R.E. and Leo Hughes owned the team, but they were businessmen. They had no time to spend running the organization. I looked around and shook my head slowly. It certainly wasn't what I had expected. All my promotional ideas would have to wait until the ballpark was fit to attend. No wonder so few of the townspeople had come out to the games in years past.

I tried to think of all the details which would have to be worked out by the time the ballplayers would arrive. The task seemed mountainous. *Somebody in Philadelphia must think I can do it,* I told myself. I decided to adopt that park as my own child. I'd make it what it should be, I'd make people want to come to it, and I'd sell baseball to this town if it was the last thing I ever did. From that second on I never looked back. I was scared of the responsibility, but the fear of failing motivated me to eighteen-hour days, seven days a week.

Everything took a backseat to the ballpark. No dating, no church, no socializing. I worked on that field from dawn to dusk, cutting grass, getting a new press box built, refurbishing the locker rooms, moving soil, painting the outfield wall and the rest rooms. Ah, the rest rooms. Guys don't care where they rest, but the ladies' room would be a masterpiece. I got some carpenters and we really did a job on it.

We air-conditioned it, painted it, wallpapered it, put in curtains and red carpeting and full-length mirrors, piped in music, hired an attendant, and arranged for fresh flowers for every game. It became our pride and joy. Whenever we showed anyone our ballpark, even the commissioner of major league baseball, the first place we took him was to the ladies' room.

In the meantime I had to do a selling job on the city fathers. We needed some financial and moral support from city government to make the thing go. There were programs to be printed, advertising space to be sold, tickets to be printed and sold, uniforms readied, and promotions lined up. I couldn't wait until all the other details were out of the way so I could get started on promotion.

I called my old sportscasting buddy from Bloomington, John Gutowsky, to see if he was interested in being the Spartanburg Philly announcer. (He had meanwhile changed his name to John Gordon.) John agreed and became my roommate for the next four years.

I also needed help in the office. I put out the word that the club needed a secretary, but got no bites until two days before the season started. At an open house for the ballplayers a local woman took me by the arm. "I heard through the grapevine that you needed a secretary," Claire Johns said. "Is the job still open?"

"Yeah," I said. She didn't look like a secretary, though I don't know what I had expected. She was a big, middle-aged gal.

"I'd like to talk to you about it," she said. We talked. I didn't have any choice. She didn't type or file or have any experience. But I had to hire her. I needed somebody, anybody. As it turned out, I never could have run the club without her. She freed me up to really do my thing. She took care of the details so I could promote. I nicknamed her Mama Johns, and she worked with me for four years. She was really a terrific woman.

As the ballpark took shape and opening day neared, Mister R.E. stayed in touch almost every day. He gave me the invaluable impression that he really believed in me. He thought I was the greatest and he told me so in his own humble way. After each of those pep talks I was so high

I wanted to go out and sell every seat in the house as a season ticket. He really kept me going. He seemed to notice everything I did right and somehow knew that I would learn from my own mistakes without his pointing them out to me. He wanted me to learn and he wanted me to succeed. I grew to love him like a father. I still do.

I was just as lady-minded as the next guy, but opening day approached and I was suddenly success-oriented. It just had to go well. I wanted to stir up publicity, fill that stadium, and run a winning team. When I saw what I had done in completely face-lifting the park, I thought I could do just about anything. If I picked my shots carefully and really made some noise in this town, I'd be in the big leagues in a matter of a few years—maybe even one year!

My mind zeroed in on that goal and I was interested in absolutely nothing else. If I could succeed at making something of this nearly deceased franchise, I wouldn't have to work at socializing anyway. People would know Pat Williams. Sure, I'd push the ballclub. Sure, I'd make it fun and exciting in the tradition of Bill Veeck. But just look at the fringe benefits—success, popularity, status. There was no stopping or even hesitating now. Pick those shots. Aim for the big one: the majors.

The first game was going to have a gigantic kickoff. Get this: The Greenville Mets were our opponents. We borrowed a goat and named him "Greenburg" after each of our teams. The loser of the opener had to keep the goat for the whole season. But the promotion that wasn't announced would be the best. Oh, Williams, you're a genius. I had contracted a skydiver. No one knew except a few of us.

Before the game he would parachute from a plane above the field. We'd quickly turn the lights out so he wouldn't hit a live wire on the way down, then we'd turn 'em back on as he neared the field. It was going to be so beautiful.

It would have been smarter if I had at least warned

the other team that the lights were going off. Dick Selma, who later pitched for the Mets and Cubs and Phillies in the majors, was warming up on the sidelines when the lights went off. He had just released a fast ball. Everyone in the stands screamed with delight, as crowds do when the lights suddenly go out. But that poor warmup catcher! He hit the ground protecting his face with his mitt, and the ball whizzed past his ear. Had it hit him on the head, I'd have killed a ballplayer before the season even started.

At the prearranged moment I flicked the lights back on so Dick Montgomery, the skydiver, could see where to land. But I didn't see him. No one knew why I had cut the lights, and with no skydiver in sight someone was going to have to come up with an excuse. Then I saw him. He was floating into the trees beyond the outfield! My blood ran cold. I hadn't killed a catcher, but I still had a chance for a skydiver.

I tried to make light of it by having our P.A. man announce, "Mr. Montgomery, your tickets are waiting if you want to get into the ballpark tonight." When he came walking in, unhurt, I could have hugged him. What a night.

I'll never forget the day we scheduled a big league exhibition game at Duncan Park. The Phillies had agreed to come in and play the Pirates, and the park was filled. I hadn't realized how many towels big leaguers use, but after batting practice word came from both batboys that the teams needed more.

There was no way that I could order another supply on a Saturday, so Claire sent the batboys to her house to round up some towels. Every one of her good, colored, hand and bath towels wound up in those grubby locker rooms!

As the stadium filled up it appeared as if we might have to rope off the outfield and let some of the fans sit inside the fence. I was so harried with all the other details that when Claire came to ask me what to do about rope, I curtly replied, "Claire, I don't care what you do. Get a thousand yards of rope if you want!"

An hour later, just as the game was about to start, Claire came to me. "Pat, the man is at the gate with the thousand yards of rope. Do you want to pay him for it?" As it turned out we didn't need any of it. At worst we would have needed about 100 yards anyway. I traded the poor guy some tickets to cool him off, but I still kid Claire whenever I see her about the day she bought enough rope to hang the whole team.

We received good publicity that season, and the fans seemed to enjoy themselves. Even though we wound up having to buy three "Greenburgs" that season (one died and another ran off), most of the later promotions were successful. The team played poorly, but we drew 114,000 fans in sixty home dates.

On the Fourth of July I had planned to treat the night game fans to a fireworks display after the game. I hadn't figured on the game going into extra innings. By the time we fired off the show, it was well after midnight. The police department and the mayor's office received so many calls from irate Spartanburgers that a city ordinance was passed the next day: no fireworks after ten P.M.

Later that month we brought in Satchel Paige to pitch a few exhibition innings. The old Hall of Famer gave me fits when he was the very last passenger to step off the plane. I was sure he wasn't going to show up. What a relief it was to see him.

Ol' Satch, the ageless wonder, whizzed through our batting order, striking out several players and allowing just one hit and no runs. The crowd loved it, and so did Satchel. He signed a photo for me, "Best wishes to Pat Williams from Satchel Paige, who would love to pitch in Spartanburg." He enjoyed himself so much he didn't want to leave.

The parent club in Philadelphia was pleased with our

season, and I was named Executive of the Year in the Western Carolinas League. I would have been happier only if I hadn't been so sure I deserved it. By this time I had made a name for myself in town. Everyone was pleased with the new look at the ballpark. They felt sorry for me because the team didn't play as well as the front office promoted. I was the child prodigy, the whiz kid, the sophisticate. And I knew it. I was twenty-five years old and thought my next step was the presidency of the Yankees or something. I really did.

I didn't have any offers or any plans, but I was convinced that the big leagues would be calling any day. Spartanburg had been fun and it had been good experience for the Kid, thank you. When a ballplayer has a good year, he moves up. The same for an executive, right? I expressed my appreciation to Mister R.E. for all his help and counsel and encouragement as we talked in his car the night the season ended.

"Patience is the key word, Pat," he said, sensing my confidence and eagerness to move on. "You've had a very good year, a very successful year, and I'm proud of you. The club has come a long way and this town is interested in baseball again. I'd like to see us get a better team in here and put that together with some good promotion." I was thinking that that would be nice for whoever the *new* G.M. would be. I had sure paved the way and made *his* job easier. Mister R.E. continued. He realized that he was going to have to be candid.

"Patience, Pat. Frankly, you are far from ready to move on. This year could have been a lot better. Anyone can have a one-shot success. The measure of real success is how well you can build. You should stay and prove yourself. Show the league and the Phillies what you're made of."

We talked for a couple of hours. I was crushed. The last thing in the world I expected was to have Mr. Little-john pop my balloon. It hurt, and it took a couple of days

to hit me that he was right. There were no calls from the
big leagues. I commuted to Winston-Salem that fall and
winter to broadcast the Wake Forest football and basketball games, and with each lonely drive across the state I
vowed to make the 1966 Spartanburg Phillies franchise the
most successful in the history of minor league baseball.

I didn't lose any respect for Mr. Littlejohn, but I
wanted as much to show him as to show the town, the big
leagues, the entire baseball business how a club should
be run. I was good enough to be in the big leagues, and I
was going to prove it. I was no longer content to take
advantage of my youth and my breaks; I was going to call
the shots, make the breaks, and move upward. I had a
mission, and I would not be stopped. I wanted nothing
short of having *The Sporting News* choose me Minor
League Executive of the Year. Getting the Western Carolinas League award was nice, but it was too local. I wanted
national recognition.

I called Bill Veeck to tell him about the season. "It was
a bit disappointing," I told him. "The club didn't win many
games."

"How many did you draw?" he asked.

"One hundred fourteen thousand."

"How many more followed the team on the radio?"

"Thousands more, I guess."

"How else could you entertain so many people? You
are in the entertainment business. Don't ever apologize
for it. Compete hard for that entertainment dollar."

We talked for quite a while that night, and Bill left
me with advice I've never forgotten. During the years
since he has added tidbits now and then, but the most
basic points were made that night on the phone. Bill was
the one who encouraged me to be totally accessible to
the fans by not screening my mail or phone calls. "Show
your fans that you're not just out for their money, but that
you care for them and want them to have a good time.

Stand at the exits after the game and thank them for coming. You want to make fans out of the new spectators."

The Wake Forest football season was over by December. It wasn't too early to begin preparing for the baseball season. I had a two-month head start over the previous season, so this year had to be better. I thought I had given my all in 1965, but now I even amazed myself. I threw myself into the running of the club and narrowed my vision until success for Pat Williams was all I could see or care about. *Sporting News* award, here I come.

The Phillies sent a good bunch of ballplayers our way. I'd have taken credit for that too if I could have figured a way. By opening day, everything was set and I was champing at the bit. That season we had a Miss Spartanburg Phillies pageant, watermelon-eating contests, find-the-lucky-number-under-your-seat games, barbecues, cow milking contests, luaus, limbo dancers, donkey baseball games, the Indianapolis Clowns, the King and His Court softball team, the Queen and Her Maids—you name it, we had it.

We even had a barnyard scramble. Our team chased farm animals all over the field to the delight of the crowd. People couldn't believe what we were coming up with. They had to come out just to find out what would be next. We had egg-tossing contests, musical chairs, and tugs-of-war. And we had a drawing for a big vacation trip.

It was magic. Everything worked. Everything. The team was great and won both halves of the season in torrid races with the Greenville Mets. They won twenty-five straight games during one stretch and the town loved it.

We had "Pack 'Em In for the Commissioner Night" and came up with a crowd to honor Baseball Commissioner Eckert. Then we had "Impress Bill Veeck Night" when he visited. At another game we had a little guy named Henri LaMothe who climbed a forty-foot ladder and dived into just sixteen inches of water. That didn't seem like much of a cushion, but it sure looked like a lot of water when he splashed it all over the infield. We had to delay the start of the game fifteen minutes until it dried!

In April the Phillies assigned two rookie pitchers to Spartanburg. It was beautiful—built-in promotion. Their names were John Parker and John Penn. It took about two seconds for a "Parker–Penn Nite" to pop into my head. I contacted the Parker Pen Company and they supplied us with hundreds of giveaway pens. I even tried to get the *Inkspots* to sing. Armed with boxfuls of pens and a pair of pitchers with appropriate names, the big night was scheduled. Parker and Penn would start either end of a doubleheader. Then the problems began.

On game day, Parker was drafted into the army. Penn's wife had a baby. And the doubleheader was rained out. We gave the pens away two days later.

One of the best promotions we put on that year involved Ron Allen, younger brother of Dick Allen, first baseman of the Chicago White Sox. Ron was our first baseman and was named the outstanding player for the month of June in the Western Carolinas League. We had a Ron Allen Night for him and I tried to fly his mother in from Wampum, Pennsylvania. There was a plane strike going on at that time, so we abandoned the idea.

The morning of the game I got a call from Mrs. Allen. "Where are you?" I asked.

"At the Spartanburg bus station." Mrs. Allen had ridden a bus all night to get to Spartanburg in time for Ron Allen Night. I arranged for a hotel room for her and told her to stay there all day and not to tell anyone she was in town. At game time we sent a police car to pick her up. While we were making presentations to Ron, the squad car pulled out onto the field and out jumped his mother. Many people cried as they embraced.

"Wouldn't you know it," Ron said. "You're only in this town one day and the police have already got you!"

I drove a big Toronado and wore sharp clothes. I had made it. I had arrived. I reveled in my success. I, I, I. I was all I cared about. No one noticed my self-centeredness. No one knew that I wanted the *Sporting News* award just for the recognition. They didn't notice my ego trip, because part of being a success at my business was being a generous, outgoing, gregarious guy. It was part of working diligently and paying the price. I was willing to sacrifice to reach this level of notoriety. It paid off. The Spartanburg Jaycees named me their Outstanding Young Man of the Year, and I was named one of the outstanding young men in the United States.

In spite of my motives that year, I had done a great job. The club did have the best, or one of the best, seasons any minor league club has ever had. I had achieved my goals. We had packed the fans in every night, and we had won the championship without even having to bother with a playoff. Once again I was named Executive of the Year by the league.

The parent club was aware of the job I had done for two seasons. In September I got a call from Bob Carpenter himself. He said the Phillies were planning to start a new team in a double-A league in Reading, Pennsylvania. He wanted me to come to Philadelphia to discuss taking over the operation of the club.

It may have been a step to a higher level of the minors, but Mr. Littlejohn had convinced me that I didn't need to move to the majors by steps. He said I could learn and build and develop recognition by staying where I was. "You can learn just as much here to prepare you for the big leagues as you can learn anywhere else," he said. I called Bill Veeck and he tended to agree with Mr. Littlejohn.

Besides, I didn't want to go to Reading. Who knew what the reception would be like? Spartanburg was a sure thing. I would have to start over at Reading.

I should have felt flattered and honored that the position was offered. I did feel important being flown to Philadelphia just to turn down a "promotion." But I did not handle it the way I should have, and I still cringe to even think about it. My actions were simply an indication of how heady my success had been. I must have believed that I was a gift to the Phillies and to baseball.

In the executive offices at Connie Mack Stadium in Philadelphia I met with owner Bob Carpenter, general manager John Quinn, farm director Paul Owens, and my old pal, Ruly. (He was on his way up in the Phillies executive chain.) Bob Carpenter did the talking. He told me they were pleased with my progress and that they would like to offer me the Reading position as their vote of confidence.

In what had to be the most cocky, arrogant, bush-league presentation of all time, I told this elite group of baseball executives that I didn't need their Reading. "I'm not about to jeopardize my career by getting myself mixed up in that town. Who knows if it's solid? I'm not going to go." I came off horribly. I should have graciously thanked them and begged off, explaining that I had made a total commitment in Spartanburg for the 1967 season; but I had to play the big shot.

I knew from the eyes darting about the room that I had incensed Bob Carpenter. In my arrogance I wasn't aware just how ridiculously I had acted. A few months later I would be told in no uncertain terms, but at that point I was so anxious to hear about the *Sporting News* award that I wasn't seeing things for what they were. The winner's name would be published in November. I could hardly wait.

November came and Mr. Littlejohn called. He invited me to his house and sat me down on the couch. "Pat," he began slowly, "word just came that the *Sporting News* award went elsewhere." Had anyone but Mister R.E. told me I would not have believed him. But he isn't the type to joke. I was wiped out.

"We have to learn to accept these things and not let them affect us," he said. "You just have to work harder." He was being kind, but I was bitter. Inside I hated the world. Everyone was against me—and they were wrong. Here I had worked my head off to draw 173,000 fans in a town of 46,000 and what did I get? I never considered the fact that *The Sporting News* consults with the parent club in choosing the winners. My arrogant act in Philly could have cost me the award.

But rather than take a what's-the-use attitude, I regrouped and vowed once more that if anyone ever deserved the award I would deserve it for 1967. (Late in 1966 our ballclub did receive the Larry MacPhail Promotional Trophy, which is presented by the National Association of Minor League Clubs.)

In December I was home visiting Mother. Mr. Carpenter asked that I visit him at his home. I had known the man since I was seven years old, and I had been almost a junior member of his family. I had stayed overnight at his house, gone on vacations with his family—everything. He had given me my start in baseball and all my subsequent breaks. But now something was wrong. My haughtiness in Philadelphia had driven a wedge between us which was still there three months later. "You are not the same young man I sent to Spartanburg two years ago," he said. "What in the world have they been feeding you down there?"

He was nailing me, and rightfully so. I was scared and I felt terrible. I said nothing. When I got back to Spartanburg I talked it over with Mister R.E. and he took much of the blame. On several occasions he told Bob Carpenter that he felt responsible for my attitude because of the counsel he had given. I wrote a long letter of apology which I heard later had been appreciated. But I believe that my turning down their promotion—or at least turning it down in the disgusting manner that I did—ended my chances of movement within the organization. It was never said, but huge corporations are run the same way. The man who turns down the European transfer may not be fired, but he may find himself categorized and bottled in the same job for years. It's only fair; I deserved it.

The following season was another success in Spartanburg. I spent about $10,000 for promotions, bringing in everyone from Bart Starr to Johnny Unitas and Paul Hornung, Oscar Robertson, Satchel Paige, and Bob Feller. I don't spend a fifth of that much in promotion *now*. I learned hard lessons trying to buy spectators. You can't do it. Any celebrity for whom you pay more than a hundred dollars or so will never draw enough extra fans to make it worth the money. Mister R.E. let me learn for myself. But I was buying myself an award. And it worked. I was named the Outstanding Class A Minor League Baseball Executive of 1967 by *The Sporting News*. We drew over 145,000 people and won both halves of the season, but the organization had very little profit at the end of the year. I had spent it buying myself that award.

5

The Gingerbread Man

I'd had about as much success in my field as a person my age could have had, but for some strange reason achieving my goals was not satisfying me.

I had always thought that all I needed were goals to strive for and to achieve so that I could move on to more challenging pursuits. If momentum and the excitement of success couldn't make me happy, what could? I was discovering that, within a few days after each triumph, the satisfaction had faded as quickly as the newspaper clippings. I was back where I had started. I had to follow my last act. What new goals could I set? My life was a real roller-coaster existence—up with the good days, down with the bad. I felt like the nursery-tale character, the Gingerbread Man, who cried out constantly,

> Run, run, run
> As fast as you can,
> You can't catch me—
> I'm the Gingerbread Man.

It was a superficial, frustrating, and selfish life, but I couldn't see it. All I knew was that it left me feeling empty.

The 1967 season had been a weird one for me. I had been named president of the ballclub, and the town had chosen me to head the March of Dimes drive. I enjoyed the popularity, but I hardly considered myself a philanthropist. If anyone was, it was Mr. Littlejohn. I was forming a higher opinion of him every day. The only time I even thought about religion or church or Christianity was when he was around. Since we were friends, I told him something very personal one day. "You are the kind of man that Christ must have been," I said. I know that sounds like quite a compliment, but the man astounded me. It embarrassed him, and he said something about the fact that no man could be compared with Christ. He seemed absolutely immune to anger or vengeance. To me he personified Christianity, but I was blind to the source of his power. I wanted to be like him the way a monotone wants to be a soloist. *I'm just not that kind of a guy*, I told myself.

Anyway, I was an all-right guy. Sure, I had a temper. Once, when a man was late delivering some ponies for a promotion, I smashed the glass on my desk top with a bat. But I was honest and didn't have any bad habits. I didn't drink booze, smoke cigarettes, kick dogs, beat little old ladies, chew tobacco, or date girls who did. I just knew God was grading me "on the curve," and I was doing a little bit better than the fellow next to me. As long as my "goods" outweighed my "bads," I honestly felt God would be pleased with me when my number was called. It was strictly a performance thing with me, and I was working it as hard as I could.

I'm sure this philosophy of life I had adopted would not have been jolted had it not been for all the "Christians" I ran into that year. In April of the '67 season, the Phillies sent Bobby Malkmus, the former big league utility infielder, to Spartanburg to help out some of the young ballplayers for a month or so. I was glad to have him come because of his connection with the big leagues and the resulting attendance draw, but I worried about the label he carried. *Religious.* That scared me a bit. I didn't know exactly what it meant. All we needed was some Bible-toting religious fanatic to turn off all the fans.

By this time I had decided that church would be a good thing to work into my schedule, not for my benefit as much as for the benefit of the ballclub and the fans. I seldom went to the same church twice, trying to move around so everyone in town would see me out now and then. Church itself meant nothing to me, but it was a good social and business move. If they thought Williams was a good guy, more churchgoing businessmen might buy ads in the program. But I wasn't sure what to expect from a guy like Bobby Malkmus. I half expected him to try to convert me the minute he showed up.

He didn't. Bobby was sharp and happy and seemed to know where he was going in life. It didn't surprise me that he wasn't a tobacco-spitting beer drinker like a lot of former big leaguers I had met, but he *was* a little more radiant than I had expected. I had the idea that he was going to be a bit syrupy and square, but I found him a delightful gentleman. And I respected his baseball savvy. He really knew his stuff. At times I almost wished that he *would* discuss his philosophy of life with me, but for the time being he was content to let his actions do the talking. They spoke loudly.

Take, for instance, the Saturday morning I got a call from the Spartanburg police department telling me that there had been some serious trouble in a tavern the night before. Three of our ballplayers had beaten up a young businessman. The players involved had left with the team for a road trip that morning, so I spent much of the day talking with the parent club in Philadelphia and leaving messages for our manager, Dick Teed, at Lexington, North Carolina.

The Phillies took a hard line with the ballplayers, ordering Teed to send them back to Spartanburg where I was to give two of them their outright releases and fine and suspend the other. Dick called me the next day and told me that they were on a bus and would arrive at Duncan Park at six-thirty P.M. Sunday.

I had dinner Sunday evening with Bobby to fill him in on the developments. He could see that I was very nervous about meeting these players. Besides the fact that it's never easy to tell a kid his baseball career is over before it had really started, I was frankly afraid of two of these guys. They were pretty tough boys. They had torn up a bar and beaten a man to a pulp two nights before, and now they had been kicked out of baseball. Who knew what they might do to me?

Bobby, who customarily went to church on Sunday evenings, changed his plans that day. He saw my need. "I'm staying with you," he said. "I'll go to the park and meet the guys with you, if that's all right." I could have hugged him.

A few minutes after we got to the ballpark, a taxi pulled up and three guys stepped out. They looked shaken, defeated. They may have been tough but being punished so severely had shellshocked them. Now I had another problem. I didn't need Bobby for protection as I had feared. I needed something to say. I felt very uncomfortable as they approached. Bobby stepped right up to meet them.

As I watched, he put his arms around the two who had been cut from the team. "I'm so very sorry, fellas," he said. "I feel terrible for you, and I want you to let me know if there's anything I can do." Of course, there was nothing he could do. He gave them no indication that he thought the punishment had been too severe, but neither did he lecture them on the fact that they had gotten exactly what they deserved. He simply was a friend when they most needed one. He had stayed home from church to meet my need, and then he had reached out immediately to meet theirs. It left me bewildered. Here was another Littlejohn, another seemingly selfless man.

Claire Johns was a sweet, Christian woman. In May, on my birthday, she pulled off the nicest surprise I've ever had. She threw a "This Is Your Life" birthday party for me and brought in my mother and sisters, Bill Durney, my cousins and aunts and uncles, and several old friends. I was flabbergasted—and impressed by a woman who really cared about me.

That same month, I was hit from another direction by the Christians. I heard some religious talk from the most unlikely guy I could have imagined. And when it was over, I realized that he had not used the word *religion*. He was talking about a person.

The man was Paul Anderson. I had once seen him put on an amazing show of strength, so I asked him to appear at our May 18, 1967, ballgame. He had never been a side act, nor had he ever played second fiddle to a ballgame, so he wrote back to inform me that he'd only do it for five hundred dollars plus expenses. I learned later that he had not expected to hear from me again. But he did. We wanted him, so we paid. And he came.

First he drove a nail through two one-inch planks with his bare hand. It was unbelievable, but each stunt topped the last. Then he lifted eighty-five-pound dumbells in each hand, using only his little fingers, and held his arms outstretched for several seconds. That warmed him up enough to press a 250-pound barbell over his head eight times. Then he was ready for the big one. We had rigged up a special wooden platform to his specifications. He called out our eight heaviest ballplayers and sat them on the platform. All weighed more than two hundred pounds, and the platform must have made the total weight more than a ton.

Paul got beneath the platform, shifted around until it was balanced evenly on his shoulders, and then hoisted the whole thing off the ground. The crowd went bananas. It was incredible. (I'm no weakling, but I couldn't lift even the empty platform when I tried after the game!)

He was an immense man, five-foot-nine and 375 pounds. He ignored the field mike we had set up and spoke for a few moments to the crowd of about 2,200 in his own booming voice. "I've lifted more weight than anyone in the history of mankind," he said, emphasizing the last syllable of every two-syllable word. I was happy with the show, but I thought he was coming off a bit egotistical at this point.

"I once lifted over six thousand pounds in a back lift," he continued. "I've been declared a wonder of nature from the United States to Russia. I've been written up in Ripley's *Believe It or Not*. I've stood on the center platform at the Olympic Games. They call me the strongest man in the world." By now I was thinking, *Boy, what a conceited guy we've got here. At least the lifting was entertaining.*

"But I want you to know, ladies and gentlemen," he went on, "that all of these things are secondary in my life." *What now?* I wondered. "I, Paul Anderson, the strongest man who ever walked the face of the earth, can't get through a minute of the day without Jesus Christ!" *What?* I was incredulous! "The greatest thing in my life is being a Christian. If I can't make it without Christ, how about the rest of you?"

The crowd was caught off guard. But this was a church-oriented town. A split second later they gave Paul the warmest ovation I had heard there in a long time. His message had done little to me or for me, but I was impressed that a guy with that kind of background would have the guts to say something like that. He didn't *have* to say anything. He could have performed his feats and gone home. I remember thinking that, even if I felt the way he did about religion, I couldn't have bared my soul like that in front of all those people. That's when it hit me. He hadn't said anything about religion. He had talked about Christ.

I had had a picture taken when I first met him, so I asked if he'd drop by the office and sign it on his way home. The photo shows me trying to lift him from behind. He signed it, "To Pat, your friend in Christ, Paul Anderson." After he left I framed it and showed it to Claire

Johns. "Look at that, Mama," I said, laughing, "he's my friend *in Christ.*"

She didn't like the mocking tone of my voice. "Watch what you say, young man," she said.

Paul's comments began to work on me a bit during the season. He *had* made an unusual point. If he, the strongest man in the world, couldn't make it through the day without Jesus Christ, what about me? I didn't allow myself to think about it too much, though I did start reading some books about other Christian athletes. I've always been an avid reader of sports books, and I had read about Christians before. But after hearing Anderson's talk I noticed that a similar thread tied the Christian books together.

I read the life stories of Minnesota football player Fran Tarkenton, former Alabama quarterback Steve Sloan, and New York Knick Bill Bradley. But the one that really intrigued me was a book on Bobby Richardson, former second baseman of the New York Yankees. The reason it interested me so was that he was a baseball player. Being from South Carolina, and playing until the end of the '67 season, he was really the biggest baseball name in the South. I wondered if I could get him to come for a promotion for the 1968 season. I started thinking of a way to take the financial burden off the ballclub. Maybe the churches would be interested in going in on the expenses. After all, it would be good for their young people to hear him, right?

The pastors didn't respond favorably to the idea of helping foot the bill until I checked with Joe Brooks, pastor of the Westminster Presbyterian Church. One of his members, Charlie Sanders, said that we should go one step further. "Let's start a chapter of the Fellowship of Christian Athletes here in Spartanburg and bring him in through that. Bobby's active in that organization."

Well, I was a wheeler-dealer, not an originator of religious organizations, but I figured if that was what we needed to get Bobby to our ballpark without paying, then

it was O.K. with me. Why not? We set up a couple of
luncheon meetings for December 1967 and discussed the
details. I was excited. It was like the Heart Fund or the
United Way to me. But by January and February 1968,
the season was approaching and we hadn't come to any decision on Bobby Richardson.

Coaches and businessmen and clergymen had been
meeting with us regularly, but it was frustrating. We met
on February 15 at the Piedmont Club, knowing that we
had to either do the necessary paperwork and initiate an
official chapter of the FCA or pull the plug and forget it.
All I knew was that I wanted Richardson by April, so I was
pushing a little.

John Gordon was there with me, and he didn't know
much more about the FCA than I did. There was a new
man, Rev. A. C. Walker from Griffin, Georgia. He had just
become the pastor of the First Baptist Church in Spartanburg, where Mister R.E. attended. When it came time to
nominate a chapter chairman, Reverend Walker stood. In
his thick Scottish brogue he said, "I would like to naumi-
nayte Paht Williams fer chairrrrman."

Everyone cheered, and it was unanimous. There
wasn't even a vote. It scared me a bit. I knew these men
had different reasons than I for wanting to start this FCA
chapter. I loved the guys and the get-togethers, but
now I was locked in. I graciously accepted, and my neck
was in the noose. I knew I wasn't into this Christian bit the
way most of the others were, but it was O.K. to be hooked
up with a wholesome group like that. Motherhood. Patriot-
ism. Apple pie. The FCA. That's the way I classified it.

One week later—Thursday, February 22, 1968—I went
to the Spartanburg auditorium to watch a couple of games
of the state girls basketball tournament. There was a concert upstairs with a group called the New Folk, accord-
ing to a pamphlet I had been handed on my way in. It
wasn't just a normal amateur singing group, I figured, because the pamphlet was sharp and obviously professionally

produced. By the end of the first game I felt like going upstairs to see what was happening. When I got up there the concert had just started. The group was singing *Dixie*. There were about eight guys and girls, good-looking kids. They had a real good sound too, accompanied by guitars and tambourines and such.

I enjoyed myself but decided that I'd leave during the intermission. I stood to make my way out when the break came, but the group leader said, "Please don't leave, folks, because in the second half we'd like to tell you what the Lord has been doing in our lives." That was a strange comment. I hadn't heard that before. I decided I would stay. *Besides, the kids seem so clean-cut, they obviously aren't fanatics or anything. And that cute little blonde was introduced as having gone to Northwestern Nursing School. Indiana is in the Big Ten conference too, so we've got that in common. If these kids are as personable as they seem, maybe I can get to talk with her later.*

When the second half started, the whole tempo of the songs changed. The New Folk were now singing songs about God and Christ. They took turns talking about their "faith in Christ" and "receiving Christ." It made no sense to me, but it was obviously real to them. At the end the leader announced, "We want to meet you, so stick around." Here was my chance to meet the little blonde.

"You're the one from Northwestern University's nursing school, huh?" I said as I introduced myself to Sandy Johnson. "I went to Indiana graduate school myself. . . ." I was trying to steer the conversation my way, so I could lay on her the fact that I was a big-shot minor league baseball president and general manager and all the rest. As I talked I felt lonely and depressed. It was cold and rainy in Spartanburg in February. We were between baseball seasons. I had enjoyed the acclaim of the last season until I could enjoy it no more. And now this Sandy Johnson was answering everything I said with something about "the Lord" and what "He" was doing in her life.

"You guys really have a good sound," I tried.

"Well, we have dedicated ourselves and our voices to
the Lord, and He's led us to share with everyone," she said.
I simply wasn't communicating with this girl. What was I
supposed to say, You're sharp and I'd like to go out with
you?

The lights began going out. Sandy smiled at me and
handed me a little booklet. "Read this. It'll help you," she
said. When I got back to my apartment I was really down.
I had failed in making the big move on Sandy Johnson,
and those kids with their radiance and joy had made me
feel flat and empty. They had something I didn't have,
and I hadn't really let Sandy tell me what it was. I looked
at the little booklet. On the front it said, *The Four Spiritual
Laws*.

I just had to know more about it. I saw qualities in
those kids that I did not possess. I had every kind of success I could have wanted, yet they were the ones who
were happy. Why? On a hunch, I called the Heart of Spartanburg, the motel across from the auditorium. "By any
chance is the New Folk singing group staying there?" I
asked. "Or a Sandy Johnson?" I had guessed correctly.
They rang her room. "Sandy? This is Pat Williams, the
guy who talked to you a while ago. . . . Listen, I'd really
like to talk to you again if you're available for breakfast
tomorrow morning." She said they were leaving at eleven
A.M. for their next stop. "O.K., then I'll see you at nine-
thirty." At the auditorium I had been trying to make a
move for her and she thought I had been interested in her
message. Now I *was* interested in her message, and I'm
sure by now she thought my interests were only romantic.
I did not sleep well.

In the morning, as John Gordon was waking up, I
read him the little booklet. "Listen, John," I said. "Isn't
this something? Tell me what you make of this: This says
that God loves everyone and has a wonderful plan for each
life. That's the first spiritual law, John. And it says that

man's sin has separated him from God and His plan. That's law number two. Law three says that the only way a person can bridge the sin gap between him and God is through Jesus Christ."

John was still half asleep. "What's the fourth one?" he asked.

"The fourth law says that a person has to ask Christ to take control of his life because Jesus won't force Himself upon a person. Here, listen to this verse: 'Behold, I stand at the door, and knock: if any man hear my voice, and open the door, I will come in to him, and sup with him, and he with me.'"

I had no idea, and John did not tell me, that at the same time he was wrestling with the very things that were troubling me. He had been going to church a bit, and he had heard Paul Anderson the year before, and he was in on the FCA deal. He had arranged a meeting with Reverend Walker of the First Baptist Church to find out more about Christianity for that very day. While I was seeing Sandy, he was getting ready to meet with the pastor.

Sandy and I ate at a place right next to her motel. She was a little guarded with me, probably mistaking my interest in Christianity for interest in her. I couldn't blame her after the way I had come on the night before at the concert. She carefully explained the four laws to me again, and we talked for quite a while. My heart was racing and I was terribly frustrated. I didn't know why. It had nothing to do with the girl; it was this Christianity thing. I had so many questions, but she had to leave soon.

At eleven o'clock she boarded the van with the other seven kids. They were still smiling, still bright, still cheery as the van pulled away.

There I stood. Confused and deeply troubled. I had a *Four Spiritual Laws* booklet in one hand and I waved with the other. I faked a smile, and then the singers were gone. Gone to Columbia. And my smile was gone too.

6

Upstaged

With Sandy Johnson and the New Folk on their way to Columbia, I was left with no one to talk to. And I was miserable. Those kids had something that I wanted, and I didn't even know what it was. I'd never before heard normal-looking people talk about "the Lord" so much. I thought that kind of thing was for kooks and weirdos who carried signs predicting the end of the world. But these kids were happy. I wasn't.

I tried to busy myself. On the way to the ballpark I stopped at a couple of places to try to sell some season tickets, but my heart wasn't in it. I was preoccupied. I couldn't shake the feeling of loneliness and frustration. It wouldn't have been so bad if I were feeling guilty and knew why. If only there was someone I could apologize to or help out or do something for to make myself feel better. I felt hopeless.

After lunch I puttered around in the office, still tormented. I had no peace of mind, and all I could think of were the smiling faces of those kids. At that very moment, unbeknownst to me, John Gordon was meeting with Rev. A. C. Walker in our messy apartment. "I want to know more about Christianity," John was saying.

"Let me show you this." Reverend Walker said in his Scottish accent. "Revelation Three, verse twenty, says, 'Behold, I stand at the door, and knock....'" With that John leaped from his chair.

"That's the same verse Pat Williams read to me this morning! That's the only verse in the whole Bible that has ever been read just for me, and now I've heard it twice in one day!" Reverend Walker, who had no way of knowing that I wasn't any more of a Christian than John was, probably figured that I'd been trying to share Christ with John.

By two o'clock I was good for nothing. I had to talk with someone. *Maybe Mr. Littlejohn will understand. He's a churchgoing man.* I decided to tell him exactly what had happened during the last eighteen hours and see what he had to say. I couldn't tell him what was troubling me because I didn't know. I drove to his office.

Arriving at exactly the same instant were Reverend Walker and John. John and I were surprised to see each other, and our greetings were a bit formal as we walked in. We all sat in Mr. Littlejohn's office and no one knew where to start. Reverend Walker and John were smiling at Mister R.E. and he was smiling at them. I wasn't smiling.

Finally Reverend Walker sat forward in his chair. "Mister R.E.," he said, as only he could say it, "I've got some wonderful news." His *r*'s were rolling like marbles and I was anxious for him to get to the point. "This young man over here, John Gordon, this afternoon committed his life to Jesus Christ."

It was like a splash of cold water in my face. I was jealous. *Why couldn't that have been me? I wanted that. That's it. That's what I wanted.* I was closer to Mister R.E. than John was, but now there was some kind of a bond between them. I had been beaten to the punch.

Mr. Littlejohn's eyes filled with tears. "Oh, that's wonderful," he said quietly. "That's just wonderful." I had never seen him so happy. I realized that he must be a

Christian, too. Why couldn't I have seen that in the way he lived before me for more than three years? I should have known.

They sat and talked for fifteen or twenty minutes, but I couldn't say anything. I was hurt, jealous, empty. John had the same look those kids had had. I was an outsider.

When they stood to leave, Mister R.E. and I stood too. Then they were gone and we were alone. Mister R.E. began talking to me slowly and quietly. "Pat, we've been praying for you since you came here. You could have such an impact in sharing Christ through the success you've had in athletics. How God could use you to spread his good news. You have a tremendous area of influence. You know, Pat, the same thing can happen to you that has happened to Johnny."

The man's love was washing over me. He had accepted me and cared about me when I was so arrogant and self-centered, and now he wanted me to know his Jesus. I fell into his arms, sobbing. For several minutes he just held me as I cried. I knew that God loved me. And I knew that Christ had died to take the punishment for my sin. Most of all, I knew that I needed to die to myself and let Christ take control of my life. That had been the toughest struggle of all. I hadn't been willing to let go of the reins. When I lifted my head from Mister R.E.'s shoulder, I had given up, surrendered to the love of Christ. I was a new man, and I knew it. For the first time in my life I had been freed by God's grace from the need to be somebody or something other than myself.

I stopped crying and my heart raced. I felt as if I had been scrubbed clean from the inside out. Success was no longer my god. I sat down and said, "I'm in now!" Mister R.E. chuckled. He suggested that I make an appointment with Reverend Walker so he could begin to teach me and bring me along in my new faith.

From the comment Claire Johns had made the day I mocked Paul Anderson, I somehow knew that she would know what had happened to me. I stopped at the ballpark and burst into the office. "Mama Johns, I've become a Christian!" I said. She was elated. I wanted to tell everyone. I had been made over in an instant. Then it hit me. *I've got to tell Sandy Johnson. Where did she say they were going? Columbia, South Carolina. But where in Columbia?* By now it was five o'clock. If I wanted to get to Columbia and leave myself enough time to find the New Folk, I'd have to hustle. I raced home to shower and change and I ran into John. Suddenly we were brothers. We carried on like little kids, chiding each other for not letting on that we had been interested in Christ for some time. That instant jealousy I had experienced was gone. I was so happy.

That night, the very day John received Christ, he had his first date with the girl who would become his wife. God took care of everything for him in one day!

I had to get to Columbia. As one of his first Christian gestures, Johnny let me take the first shower! As I was getting dressed, he jumped in the shower and sang out, "Oh, no, what kind of a Christian are *you?* You used up all the hot water!"

I experienced my first miracle about an hour and a half later when I cruised into Columbia with no idea where the New Folk might be. The only landmark I knew was the University of South Carolina Field House. I went there. And there they were, doing the same program they had played the night before in Spartanburg. It had meant nothing to me then, but now every word seemed to have been written and sung just for me. They were praising my Lord, and I sat there lit up like a firefly.

When the program ended I sought out Sandy Johnson. She saw me coming and I'm sure she said to herself, *This guy never gives up.* I didn't want her to get the wrong impression. I simply wanted to tell her what had happened. I said, "Sandy, everything you told me last night and this morning is very clear to me now. This afternoon I received Jesus Christ into my life."

She looked at me, beaming. "Praise the Lord," she said.

I quickly said goodnight and walked to my car. I cried all the way home.

The next day I called home to tell Mother, but I don't think I handled it too well. After raising her children in the Presbyterian Church and keeping them from lives of degradation, she couldn't understand why I would need anything more. She asked me if I was sure this wasn't some kind of an emotionally charged experience.

Well, it wasn't that, and I told her so. But as I thought about it, my experience *had* certainly been emotional. Yet I *hadn't* gotten into some kind of new religious kick. None of the Christians I had anything to do with even mentioned religion. This was a Person, a way of life. Not a religion.

Mother does admit that the "experience" was good for me, and she can't deny that I have "stuck with it." But really, God has stuck with me. I am unworthy of His love, and there's no way I can earn His favor or the gift of His Son. That's all I need to know. Years of Sunday school and church had given me everything but Jesus Christ. And now I had Him.

The next day I had an army reserve meeting, which I always dreaded. As a one-day-old Christian, I found myself even enjoying that!

The New Folk kids had told me about a retreat the following weekend in Athens, Georgia. It was to be led by a man named Hal Lindsey, a name which meant nothing to me then. I knew I wouldn't know anyone at the retreat, but I was hungry for any fellowship with other Christians, and there was so much I wanted to learn.

In Athens the next weekend I walked into a large Methodist church where dozens of college kids were milling about. No one knew Pat Williams, so I just sort of looked around. The only name I remembered was Hal Lindsey. I asked an attractive, black-haired lady if she knew where he was.

"He's around here somewhere," she said. "I'm his wife, Jan. Can I help you?"

"Well, I'm Pat Williams from Spartanburg and I've been a Christian for about a week. I'm here but I don't know why I'm here. Help me."

She kept track of me from then on, being sure I knew where to go when, introducing me to people, and generally watching out for me. I told her I didn't know where I was going to stay. "Well, you're staying with Hal and me," she said.

That weekend was the greatest thing that could have happened to me as a new Christian. Again, I was impressed that Christians are not fanatical oddballs. These kids were warm and genuine and happy and loving. I was drawn into their midst and they made me feel like a brother. If I needed anything to bolster my new faith, that was it. The Bible studies and discussions may have been a little heavy for me at that point in my spiritual life, but I ate them up. One thing I learned was that I should be totally willing to do anything God leads me to do. That was a tough lesson. I had to come to the point where I would be willing to even give up my pro sports career and be a missionary if that's what God wanted.

At first that sounded a bit unfair and disappointing. But the point wasn't that God was going to send me off somewhere I wouldn't want to go. The point was that I should be *willing* to love and serve Him to that extent. It was another emotional experience when I placed my career in His hands. I was eager to be led wherever He wanted me. That was a real switch. For several years I had been maneuvering to be seen at the right places and be written up in the strategic publications so that I could make big moves. Now I was letting God handle all that.

If He wanted me somewhere else, fine. Until then, I was content to stay in Spartanburg and tell people about Him for the rest of my life.

I couldn't seem to tell enough people. I know I probably turned off as many as I turned on with my news, but there was no stopping me. I was so excited with my fresh outlook and my peace of mind that I wanted everybody to know. And I wanted them to receive Christ too.

One Sunday the minister from the First Baptist Church in Gaffney, South Carolina, asked me to come to the joint adult Sunday school classes and share what had happened in my life. I just stumbled through it, but it was a thrill to share with a group. I had done a lot of public speaking in promoting the ballclub, and now I found promoting Christ even more fun. And people seemed to enjoy hearing it.

The Lions Club had given the ballclub a half-hour on their program one day, so I had arranged for the farm club director, Paul Owens, to speak. The day before the meeting he called to cancel out, so I was left with the half-hour program but no Paul Owens. Here was my chance to talk to the 100 or so most influential men in the community.

"I've been in this town for three years," I began. "You know me. I've spoken to you before. You know me for my involvement with the ballclub. But let me tell you what has happened in my life recently. . . ."

That little speech hit the city like a bomb. There are few secrets in a medium-sized Southern town. In a matter of days the whole town knew. One woman asked Reverend Walker, "If Pat and Johnny weren't Christians, who is?" If she had only known the depths to which I had slipped in running my own life. I was still very much in the limelight and enjoying recognition, but now I had a different motive. I was using my unique opportunities to share Jesus Christ.

The following Sunday Reverend Walker asked if I would tell my story from his pulpit at the special Youth

Sunday. It was televised so many people throughout the state saw it. After that my schedule was packed. I was asked to come to churches I had never even heard of. I didn't know the language of Christians too well, which was that much the better—I didn't get lost in clichés. I had a fresh experience with God and I was thrilled to tell of it. It seemed that I was somewhere every day, an infant Christian sharing his joy.

Reverend Walker and Mr. Littlejohn impressed upon me the importance of a daily walk with God. They told me that the emotional high might wear off and then I'd worry about the validity of my relationship with Christ. They were right. The bubbly thrill could not last forever. That would have been unrealistic. God had never promised that my becoming a Christian would insulate me against problems. Neither was there any promise that I wouldn't sometimes slip into the same selfish nature that had once ruled me.

So I read my Bible daily, never being able to get enough of what God had for me. And I prayed. What an experience. No more was it a ritual for Sunday mornings or Christian holidays. I could really talk to God. And He listened. He didn't care that I didn't sound like a great pillar of the faith or some theological giant. I wasn't embarrassed to use everyday language and ignore the *thee*'s and *thou*'s I had always associated with reverent prayer. Of course, there's nothing wrong with praying that way if it lends to a spirit of reverence; but for me, as a new Christian, my reverence was measured in faith. Daily prayer and Bible reading kept me going and believing long after the emotional high had worn off.

When we found out from the parent club that Bobby Malkmus had been chosen to be our manager for 1968, John Gordon and I couldn't wait to call and tell him what had happened. He was so happy he kept saying, "Praise the Lord." It made us really glad we had called him. He was as excited to hear about it as we had hoped he would be.

When Bobby returned to Spartanburg that spring, I think I surprised him. He asked what he should talk about at a civic luncheon I had arranged. "Just tell them about the Lord, Bobby," I said. He told me later that that was the first time he had really spoken out for Christ in public.

A stewardess I had dated a few times called me one night to see why I hadn't been around or called for a while. "Well, I've really been busy as a new Christian," I said.

"What!"

"That's right. Listen, I've found something that I didn't even know I was looking for." Now she was really confused. "I've received Jesus Christ into my life and I'm a new person. I'm happy and peaceful and excited all at the same time."

I told her the whole story of how it had come about. "I think I'd better come down there and hear more about this," she said.

When I met her at the airport a few days later, I had already told her everything I knew. It was obvious that she had more questions than I could answer. I took her to talk with Bobby Malkmus. Bobby doesn't pull any punches. He told her exactly what the Bible says about her need for a savior. He pointed out that the Bible says that everyone is born in sin and is separated from God. She got nervous after a while and asked if we could leave. Bobby hadn't turned her off. He had started her thinking about something which bothered her until the next day.

On the way back to the airport I asked if we could stop and see just one more guy: Reverend Walker. She said she'd like to. We stopped at the church office and talked for quite a while. Reverend Walker gently expounded upon the truths Bobby had shared the night before, and my friend decided that she would like to pray and ask Christ into her heart and life. I had never been so thrilled. Nothing compares with seeing someone come to Christ. I still cry when I hear that someone has turned his life over to God. We're so much more secure when we're out of our own hands and into His.

There was a real bond among the ballpark personnel in the 1968 season. The owner, the president and G.M., the manager, the radio sportscaster, and the office secretary were all Christians. We had some wonderful times. More than once Johnny and I wished aloud that we had found Christ a few years before. For all the success and fun we'd had, nothing had ever fulfilled us. Never again would I wonder, *Is that all there is?*

My eyes were no longer trained on the major leagues. It was a remote possibility, but since the desire to "make it" no longer filled every moment of my day I often went for days without even considering a future anywhere but in Spartanburg.

The team started strong that year and finished in first place for the first half of the season. It was the fifth straight half-season championship for Spartanburg, and, as Bill Veeck has always said, "The best promotion is winning." We had good crowds.

By April we had started a thriving FCA chapter (Dr. Loren Young spoke at the charter dinner), and guess who was invited to beautiful Duncan Park? That's right. Bobby Richardson. The park was packed with young people who heard Bobby say before the game, "When you receive Christ by faith, God will pardon all your sins past and present; He'll give you real peace with yourself and your neighbor; He'll give you a true purpose for living; and He'll give you the power to live up on top of your daily circumstances. Christ will never leave you nor forsake you. You never have to be afraid again."

Bobby must have signed a thousand autographs before he left the park.

It might have been easy for me to misunderstand my

responsibility as a new Christian. I suppose it could have made me less effective as a club president, had I put my job in the background. But I received valuable counsel from my more mature Christian friends. Mr. Littlejohn told me that now, more than ever, I had every reason to be the best promotional man I could be. I sought publicity and the spotlight but not for myself—for the club. And if, in the process, I got a chance to speak personally, I often shared Christ.

I was happier than I had ever been. Problems and foul-ups which once would have tied me in knots were now being taken in stride as I let Christ be my strength. It was a whole new way of life for me, and I knew I never wanted it to end. Maybe I really *would* stay in Spartanburg forever.

The Lindseys had suggested several books for me to read. I was quite a reader anyway, and when I finished the books they recommended I gobbled up any Christian book I could find. I was reading over my head, but I didn't care. I wanted to read anything that would give me more insight into the new relationship I had with Christ. I read *A Wider Place, Make Love Your Aim, The Cross and the Switchblade,* and *God's Smuggler.* I was charged up anew with each book.

By July I had spoken at least twice and usually three times a week about Christ to various groups. I was being fed spiritually by the mature Christians around me, by the First Baptist Church, and by all the books I was reading. I had a purpose in life, and things couldn't have been better. Nothing was on the horizon in my career because I hadn't been trying to work any deals or put myself in advantageous positions. Then I found that, when God is running the show, a person can get a break without having had anything to do with it. It was a new experience for me.

On July 8, 1968, I walked into the ballpark office and found a message on my desk from Claire. I was to return a call to Jack Ramsay in Inglewood, California. The only Jack Ramsay I had ever heard of was the one who had coached basketball so successfully for many years at St. Joseph's College in Philadelphia and who was then the general manager of the Philadelphia 76ers of the NBA. It couldn't be him—he didn't even know me.

But it was. I returned the call and his voice, with that unmistakable Philadelphia accent, came over the wires. "Have you been following what has been happening with our team?" he asked.

I told him I had. "I'm out here to work out the final details of our trade with Los Angeles," he continued. "We're getting Darrall Imhoff, Archie Clark, and Jerry Chambers for Wilt Chamberlain. The trade will be announced later this afternoon." I felt honored that he would let me in on the unannounced news, but I was still puzzled about why he had called. "You know our coach resigned and we haven't been able to get anyone to replace him yet," he said, "so I'm going to coach the team this season. That won't leave me much time for my general manager duties, so we're going to need a business manager. Are you interested?"

I was speechless, but I managed a "Y-yeah." It wouldn't have surprised me more if he had asked me to replace Chamberlain as the new center. I didn't even know where he had gotten my name. (He told me later, "More is known about you in Philadelphia than you might think.") He told me that he'd talk with me in Philadelphia in a few days.

For more than three years I had done everything I could to call my own shots and get myself into the major leagues of baseball. All I had wanted for six years was to run a big league club. I had never even thought of basketball, but here was the break. It was strange and so obviously from God that I didn't feel I should pass it up. No, it wasn't miraculous, but that it came after I had resigned

myself to staying in Spartanburg made me realize that the
Lord had simply waited until I was sold out to Him.

I flew to Philadelphia and Ramsay offered me a three-
year pact at $20,000 a year. It took a lot of faith for
the guy to offer to turn over the business end of the 76ers
to a twenty-eight-year-old kid whose only experience was
in the Class A minor leagues of baseball. But he did. He
was saying in effect, "I'm coaching, traveling, scouting,
and practicing, and you can reach me when you need
me. Otherwise, the business end is yours." I was to handle
everything but player personnel. I would be in charge of
promotion, publicity, ticket sales, everything for home
games. I liked the idea.

I took a cab to the Phillies offices to talk to Paul
Owens, the Phillies' farm system director. I told him what
was brewing and he asked me to wait until he had a
chance to talk to Ruly. The next day Ruly called me in
Spartanburg. "Wait a few more days," he said. "I want to
check out the 76ers front office and their owner, Irv Kosloff, to make sure everything is solid." I really appreciated
that. When he called back a few days later and said
everything seemed to check out, I made my decision.

I called Ramsay and said, "I feel good about this,
and I'm with you. I'll finish out the baseball season here
and I can join you by Labor Day."

The rest of the 1968 baseball season in Spartanburg
was tough on me. I still enjoyed myself but I could hardly
wait to get to Philadelphia. Then Ramsay called.

"I've got a problem," he said. *I've already accepted
the job*, I thought. *What now?* I couldn't speak my mind
for fear of ruining a good thing. "Mr. Kosloff would like to
talk to you before we make this official. Do me a favor and
give him a call, and I'm sure everything will work out."

I called Kosloff. "I want you to do two things for
me," he said. "First, I want you to have three people who
know you call me collect so I can talk to them about you.

Second, I want you to come to Philadelphia next Monday and go to the following address by ten o'clock in the morning." He read off the address and hung up. I was upset, but I thought maybe he was just testing me to see if I'd follow directions.

I had Bill Veeck; Vic Bubas, basketball coach at Duke; and Andy Musser, the 76ers' sportscaster, call Kosloff. And I went for the mysterious ten o'clock appointment the following Monday. It turned out to be the office of Dr. Norman Gekoski of Management Psychologists, Inc.

I was greeted and told that I had five hours of testing in front of me. By now I had had it. "I don't have five hours of testing ahead of me," I said. "What's this all about?" I almost walked out, but I wanted the job so badly that I stayed. I started the testing in an angry mood.

Then I met Dr. Gekoski. He called me into his office for an hour interview. I found him to be a superdelightful man and a good basketball fan. He would become a close friend during my season with the 76ers. It was a good thing I got to talk to him or I might have taken that bad attitude all the way through the testing.

Later that afternoon I met with Kosloff's banker, who was another of his confidants. By the time I met with Kosloff he had already gotten reports from both his banker and Gekoski, and on the way to the airport he told me that the job was mine. It had been a long, trying day, but I had certainly learned a valuable lesson in patience.

Mr. Littlejohn wanted me to stay in Spartanburg. He offered me complete ownership of the Spartanburg Phillies, a mind-boggling offer. But he knew I was going. And he encouraged me. The most important thing to him was that I had my feet on the ground, that I knew who I was, why I was here, and where I was going. I knew. I was going to a pro basketball team which had just traded away the biggest gate draw ever. We would have to draw crowds to see a team which no longer had Wilt Chamberlain. I looked forward to the challenge.

7

Don't Let the 76ers Wilt

Wilt Chamberlain had been traded to Los Angeles, and the prophets of doom had predicted that the club would never draw nearly as many fans again. My tear-filled good-bye at the Littlejohns' house was still fresh in my mind when I arrived at Philadelphia the day after Labor Day 1968. Jack Ramsay told me that he felt the club would do just fine without Chamberlain; he thought they'd play a more interesting game. They did, and that helped. In fact, Philadelphia made the playoffs before losing to Boston in the first round.

After five days or so of heavy instruction from Jack, he was gone. I saw him after that only when the team was in town. You talk about on-the-job training! I was fresh out of the South and as green as I could be. Once again motivated by fear, I dug in and worked my head off. It was good to be a Christian. The business of promoting Pat Williams was no longer in my hands. I could concentrate on my job.

There was little difference in my philosophy of promoting basketball as opposed to baseball. In basketball the shows are scheduled for halftime instead of before the game, and the challenge is to keep people entertained during the intermission. Of course I want to give them time to hit the rest rooms and the concession stands, but we don't want them to remember sitting for fifteen or twenty minutes with nothing to see or do.

Rather than trying to fill a 5,000-seat minor league baseball stadium, I was now working in a place that would hold more than 15,000 but which had never averaged over 9,000 for a basketball season. That seemed ominous until I remembered that, if I had been in major league baseball, I'd be worrying about filling 50,000 seats for more than eighty home dates.

I liked the noise in pro basketball, too. Basketball stadiums are enclosed, of course, so the noise echoes and re-echoes. There's nothing like an overtime game with a full house of screaming fans to blow the roof off a stadium. It really gets wild. I decided to attack the season game by game. The 76ers had forty-one home dates scheduled. We needed just the right promotion for each one. When the leading teams would visit we could experiment with some new acts or try something goofy. The fans would come out for the game anyway. And when the losing teams were in town, we'd pull out all the stops. If fans don't care to see a lousy team, maybe they'll come for the halftime show and find that the game was exciting anyway.

One night early in the season we had scheduled a doubleheader. The Knicks would play in the first game, and the 76ers would play in the second. The games would have been enough to bring most fans out, but I decided that this would be a good time to really unload with some good shows. At halftime of the first game we featured Victor the Wrestling Bear. Any fan who dared grapple the 700-pound beast would get a couple of free tickets to the next ballgame. And anyone who beat him would win some cash. I don't remember how much we offered because we never worried about losing it. Victor, who is

declawed and defanged and muzzled, has such strength
in his massive arms that no one had a chance. Even 275-
pound pro football players have been pinned in seconds
by Victor.

The New York sportswriters were in to cover the
Knicks and they got a big charge out of Victor. A few
fans tried knocking him down, but he handled them easily
and it was hilarious. A photo and story made the front
page of the *New York Daily News.*

For halftime of the second game I had asked Dick
Allen, then a superstar third baseman for the Philadelphia
Phillies, to bring his rock group, Dick Allen and the
Ebonistics, to the Spectrum. Dick had been in the middle
of controversy in town, but the music was great and the
fans ate it up. The publicity really started to pick up and
the 76ers were fast becoming known for more than just
good basketball.

The most incredible show I have ever been involved
with came my way from one of the players. One of our
guys had heard of a girl named Arlene whose thing was
eating. He said she helped promote the opening of a ham-
burger stand by eating hamburgers there all evening. It
sounded a bit unbelievable to me, and I had visions of
some porky slob who would get laughed out of the stadium. But I called her.

She sounded very sweet and dainty. She said she'd
be happy to help us with a show for just the cost of her
expenses. We could hardly lose. For a couple of weeks
we billed the coming attraction as "Little Arlene," and
we challenged the five biggest eaters in town to come to
the ballgame and try to eat more than Arlene. She claimed
she could outeat any five men put together!

A few days before Little Arlene arrived I got a long-
distance call from a guy who had been to one of our
recent games. He was vacationing in Florida and had
found four other big guys who agreed to challenge Arlene.

They called themselves the Philadelphia Fillups, featuring the Galloping Glutton. I couldn't imagine a girl outeating five healthy college guys, but we started advertising in earnest.

When the big night came we had quite a crowd. The eating was to begin at seven o'clock and continue through the ballgame until we had a winner. Arlene said she had no preference as to the food, so we agreed upon hotdogs without the buns, medium pizzas, and Cokes. The food was brought out by stadium personnel dressed as chefs. Little Arlene, who really was little, began very slowly and daintily. She was not a slobbery lady. The guys started horsing down hotdogs and pizzas and Coke.

By eight o'clock the guys had slowed down. Each had eaten a couple of medium pizzas and about fifteen hotdogs with several Cokes. But it wasn't a speed contest. This was for quantity. Arlene was still munching away, showing not the least sign of fatigue. The crowd began to really take notice.

A little after eight, the guys were through. They were sitting, standing, lying, walking slowly, and drinking glassfuls of Alka-Seltzers. They looked green. Arlene—skinny little persevering Arlene—was still eating. If I hadn't seen it with my own eyes, I'd have never believed it. I hardly expect you to believe it either. That girl, in slightly less than three hours, personally chewed up and swallowed seventy-six hotdogs and twenty-one medium pizzas and drank twenty-five Cokes.

"Is that enough?" she asked politely. I assured her that it was quite enough and announced that she had totally wiped out the Glutton and Company. Then she casually ate two more hotdogs to run her total to seventy-eight and looked completely bored. Basketball didn't interest her. "Could you announce," she asked me, "that I will challenge any five people in the stands to a fish-eating contest at Bookbinder's seafood place after the game?" I announced it, but no one volunteered. I understand she went anyway and enjoyed a big meal.

The Little Arlene story didn't end until a few days later when we got the bill for the hotel room we had provided. One of the items she had charged was a full roast beef dinner about an hour before the eating contest at the Spectrum! Until I see a baby outwrestle Victor the Wrestling Bear I doubt that I'll ever see a show so incredible as Little Arlene and her gigantic appetite.

The Spectrum personnel, ushers, ticket-sellers, maintenance men, security guards, everybody began getting caught up in the fun of the season. Nothing is more satisfying to me than to see the team and the people involved with the club take pride in the good times we offered. In my mind a basketball franchise has about three hours to sell at each game. Something has to be going on all the time. It's tough, and it's demanding, but there's no substitute for it. A person has to remember an entire night of entertainment or he'll never be back. I want them all back.

I'm not running a circus, and I'm not a clown, but I'm sure in the same business. Clowns like to see people forget their troubles and laugh and enjoy themselves. I would rather be remembered as a good businessman, a good basketball talent scout, a good diplomat and negotiator. But I know that, when it's all been said and done, people will remember me for Victor and Little Arlene. That's O.K. If it weren't for promotions like that, the ballclubs I've worked for wouldn't have had any money for me to manage, and I'd have been out of a job a long time ago. Many people don't realize that a lot more goes into running a ballclub than having a crazy halftime show lined up. But they don't need to know more than that—as long as they enjoy themselves and come back.

As I became closer to Irv Kosloff, I found him a valuable tutor. "Ask yourself two questions every hour of the day," he would often say. "First: What am I doing to help the team win more games? And second: What am I doing to help the team draw more fans? That's all that matters. Don't get yourself bogged down with meaningless details." I still follow that advice.

I had been chairman of the Fellowship of Christian Athletes chapter in Spartanburg before I was even a Christian, so by the time I knew what it was really all about I was on my way to Philadelphia. As a six-month-old Christian, I needed a group like the Philadelphia FCA for spiritual food. They met my need. For several months I worked with them and helped them plan special events and so forth. I looked and looked for a good home church, but nothing compared with First Baptist in Spartanburg. I wanted a place with a solid, friendly pastor like Reverend Walker; but maybe I had set my sights too high. I read more and more Christian books and started spending a lot of time with FCA worker Ted Deinert. (Ted later married Billy Graham's daughter, Bunny.)

Ted and I worked on an FCA banquet for May 1969. The basketball season would be over by then and I would be free to really help get some personalities who would add a touch of class to the big banquet. It was a success. We invited every Christian athlete we could think of in the area, and they all showed up. My mother and my uncle even drove up from Wilmington, so the whole banquet was a highlight for me.

I was thoroughly enjoying myself in Philadelphia. The *Sporting News* had done a full-page story on the promotions I had done for the 76ers, Jack Ramsay was happy, and, most of all, owner Irv Kosloff was pleased. I had two more years to go on my contract and had found myself a willing convert from baseball to basketball. I was captivated.

The summer months kept me busy representing the ballclub at speaking engagements around town. I found more and more opportunities to talk about Christ. He never said so personally, but I read once that 76er Darrall Imhoff said he was challenged to bring his faith in Christ out of hiding after hearing me boldly share my experience. That humbles me. The only boldness I had then or have now to share Christ so freely comes from God.

In late July we were preparing for training camp which would open the next month. Then Bill Veeck called. A friend of his, Phil Frye of Chicago, wanted to talk with me. Frye had been one of Veeck's stockholders when Bill had owned the Chicago White Sox. Now Frye was one of eight owners of the Chicago Bulls basketball team. I had no idea what Frye would want to talk with me about, but I was curious enough to call.

Frye told me that Dick Klein, one of the other Bull owners, had been acting as general manager. The team was at rock bottom, making no money, drawing few fans, and little help was in sight. Frye said the owners agreed that changes would have to be made. "We want to know if you'd be interested in at least talking to us about being the general manager," he said. "This is not an offer, but it may become one. We'd like you to come to Chicago to talk with us."

I was burning inside. What an opportunity! The chance to run a pro sports franchise, and a big one at that. Sure, it was sick, down, and almost dead, but it was Chicago. I wanted it. I had to control myself though. I still had two years left on my 76er contract. "Let me call you back," I told Frye.

Jack Ramsay was intrigued to learn I had been approached by the Bulls. He had been negotiating with them all summer in an attempt to get Bull forward Jimmy Washington, whom he thought could become a superstar in the right environment. He was willing to give up veteran 76er star Chet Walker for Washington, but the talks had been stalemated for weeks. The Bulls had never mentioned an interest in me during those negotiations. "Sure, go ahead and talk with them," Jack said.

I flew to Chicago for a four-hour interview with the Bulls brass. They told me the sordid details on how rough things would be in a town where baseball and football reigned supreme with the public. I discussed ways I thought Chicago fans could be sold on pro basketball and I got the impression that they liked what they heard.

I didn't know for sure until Bulls president Elmer Rich called me a week later. "We'd like to make you an offer if you'll visit us again," he said. I would have *walked* to Chicago that night if he had wanted. The Bulls offered a two-year deal at $30,000 per year. I went to Ramsay and Mr. Kosloff and asked to be released from my contract.

First they wanted to be sure that this was what I wanted. It was. I didn't see a future for myself in Philadelphia. Jack had the ballclub well in hand, and anyway I wasn't looking to move up. I hadn't even thought of Chicago. Since I was no longer in the business of fighting my way to the top, God had taken care of all my breaks for me. Mr. Kosloff had become a close friend and was reluctant to let me go. He was happy with the 10,000-plus average attendance, but he finally gave in.

Ramsay said that he would be willing to let me go on the condition that the Chet Walker for Jimmy Washington deal went through. That sounded fine with me. Chet had been a tremendous asset in Philadelphia, and, while Washington certainly appeared to have superstar potential, no one could guarantee it. "I do have to check with the Bulls coach, Dick Motta, first," I told Jack. "I wouldn't want to start off on the wrong foot by trading away one of his favorites."

Motta wasn't the biggest Jimmy Washington fan in Chicago, but he desperately wanted Chet Walker. He had not been consulted on the deal before or it probably would already have been made. When I learned that he was all for it, we pushed through the paperwork and I found myself in a fast friendship with Dick Motta. I told him that I would never make a trade without consulting him and that he would have the final word on the playing end. He had been burned badly in a few other trades, so he was happy to hear that.

I liked Motta right off the bat. He seemed shy and soft-spoken. I spent the entire evening at his suburban home the night before the press conference at which the Bulls announced my hiring. We talked for hours. He said he'd had such a terrible time under his former boss that any new G.M. would have been an improvement. He was excited about the Walker trade, so his spirits were high.

After the press conference the next day we had to talk with Jimmy Washington. He had a no-trade clause in his contract, but he didn't press it because he was from Philadelphia and looked forward to playing closer to home. Anyway, I think he must have been honored to have been traded for Chet Walker.

Chet wasn't so excited about the idea. It's not easy for an established star to take getting traded to one of the weakest franchises in the league after having played with a winner. Among other things, he had enjoyed the big crowds in Philadelphia. In Chicago the Bulls were drawing less than 5000. Chet didn't want to go.

Dick Motta and I flew to Philadelphia to talk to Chet. He wouldn't answer our knock. We knew he was there because we could hear music from inside. We went out and called him. Chet finally agreed to come down and meet with us. Dick talked to him at length, convincing him that he would work in nicely and could help turn the Chicago franchise around. I sensed that Dick hated to subject himself to anyone, but a guy like Chet Walker played Motta's brand of basketball. Dick doesn't regret begging a little to get him.

Walker became and still is one of the most important

cogs in the Chicago basketball machine. Much of their success over the past five years is directly attributable to his talent. Washington is now with Atlanta, and, while he is a fine starting forward, he never became the superstar Ramsay had hoped. It was a good trade to start my negotiating career with.

When the trade was announced, it looked, of course, like Williams had come to town and made a big deal the same day. That gave rise to a little enthusiasm, and when Dick and I worked out a few more deals within the next couple of weeks, heads started to turn. Maybe these guys in Chicago were serious. They had hired an unknown coach named Motta from a tiny West Coast college the year before. And now they had put a twenty-nine-year-old kid in charge of the club. But they *were* making some deals for good ballplayers.

I had to get an office set up, hire a staff, be sure all the players were in the fold, learn the ropes, and start lining up ticket sales and promotions. The season would start in less than a month. My head was still spinning, but the few seconds of thought I allowed myself before falling asleep each night were filled with the glorious realization that God had brought me to Chicago. He had given me the desires of my heart when I had been content to stay in Philadelphia—indeed, even stay in Spartanburg. How good could God be?

8

Jillo

I had been in Chicago just a few days as the new general manager of the Bulls when I first saw the Moody Memorial Church. It's really an impressive structure, a huge, stately old building just blocks from the Loop.

I decided that Moody Church would be a good place to begin looking for a home church. My search for a church ended the first Sunday. Dr. George Sweeting (now president of Moody Bible Institute) proved to be a pastor who preached forcefully straight from the Bible and was able to communicate on the new Christian's level. I was fascinated by this source of spiritual food and made Moody Church a habit whenever I was in Chicago on Sundays. Dr. Sweeting and I became friends and he often asked me to share my story from the pulpit.

There was no Fellowship of Christian Athletes chapter in Chicago, but not long after I arrived God led several Christians into the area. Don Shinnick and Craig Baynham came to the Bears. J. C. Martin came to the Cubs, where Randy Hundley and Don Kessinger had been for several seasons. And Jimmy King came to the Bulls. Suddenly there was a nucleus of Christian sports figures who were all interested in more outlets for sharing their faith. By the summer of 1970 we had held a small press conference to announce our intention of beginning an FCA chapter, and within another year or so many of the principals were gone. God had simply brought us together to begin a work there which continues to this day, and which is one of the strongest and most effective FCA chapters.

The Bulls did well my first season there. Dick Motta and I made some good trades and the fans started coming out. We had Boy Scouts night, and merchants night, and all kinds of crazy stunts that had worked in Miami and Spartanburg and Philadelphia. About a month into the season we drew our largest crowd up to that point, a little over 10,000 people. The Atlanta Hawks were visiting, and we were blowing them off the court. The crowd was noisy and happy. Then in the second half the Hawks caught fire: they closed the gap and kept pressing, forcing Chicago mistakes and turnovers. Finally, with just a few seconds left on the clock, the Hawks surged into the lead by two points.

Motta called a time out to set up a play. We had to get a bucket to send the game into overtime. The Bulls came back out on the floor and worked the ball to Clem Haskins. He shot. The ball bounced off the rim as the seconds ticked away and the crowd shouted and stomped. The rebound came off to big Tom Boerwinkle, who laid it in. Tie game? No. The refs' whistles were drowned out by the delirious fans. Finally they communicated. The refs claimed that time had run out and that the basket was no good—the Hawks won. Dick Motta went nuts. He charged onto the floor screaming at the refs and pointing to the old hockey clock in the rafters. It clearly showed one full second left. I had collared the other ref and was screaming at him. The players were carrying on too, and the argument lasted several minutes.

The refs claimed that they had counted the last seconds off to themselves because the noise was so great that they wouldn't be able to hear the final buzzer. They couldn't look at the clock because they didn't want to miss the action. After the stadium emptied, we turned on a tape recorder. Then we turned on the clock again. The tape recorder verified a second of silence between the click and the buzzer. A photographer had taken a picture of the clock with a second remaining. We were ready to file a protest to the league office.

No one had ever won a protest in the National Basketball Association, but we knew we were right. A protest must be accompanied by $1000, and if the protest is rejected the club loses the money. We filed. For the next two days the sports pages in Chicago's four major daily papers carried scads of stories on the protest. It may have been one of the best things that could have happened at that point in my career with the Bulls. Suddenly the whole town had a *reason* to support the Bulls.

We hosted the Boston Celtics in our next home game and I had worked out a promotional deal with Kentucky Fried Chicken. They were giving away free dinners and prizes, but it was the uproar over the protest which had really brought the fans. The Chicago Stadium holds around 19,000 people, and 13,000 showed up that night. The Bulls were so psyched up they destroyed the Celtics. I was ecstatic. A few weeks later we scheduled the Harlem Globetrotters for the preliminary to our game against the San Diego Rockets. We opened the gates and the people started coming—and they just kept coming and coming. Six weeks into the season we had filled the house for a ballgame.

A week later Kareem Abdul-Jabbar (formerly Lew Alcindor) made his first appearance in Chicago with the Milwaukee Bucks. Another full house. In December we offered free basketballs for all the kids who came. Fifteen thousand fans showed. Before the season was three months old the *dead* Chicago franchise had exploded. That early season success remains my most gratifying experience in sports promotion. The NBA commissioner's office later upheld our protest of the Atlanta game. It was replayed from the point of the protest and we lost in overtime, but felt good to be involved with the first protest ever upheld.

In February I scheduled Victor the Wrestling Bear. Our publicity man, Ben Bentley, thought it would be cute to add a teaser line to the press release, so he wrote, "Though the bear is muzzled, it has not been fed for a month." Wally Phillips, a popular madcap morning disk jockey for WGN Radio in Chicago, saw the release and thought he'd have fun with it too. He began calling housewives and telling each one that he had heard her husband was going to wrestle the bear at the Bulls game. "Is his insurance paid up?" Wally would ask. "Where would you like the body delivered?"

One thing led to another and the Anti-Cruelty Society heard about it. People began calling our offices and the ACS headquarters demanding to know why we had this trapped bear and were starving it to death. The morning of the game we received a telegram from the head of the Humane Society in Chicago informing us that bearbaiting is illegal in the state of Illinois. When the press quizzed me I didn't feel that I should treat it as a serious problem since all the fuss had been caused by mistaken impressions. "Why is everyone so worried about this huge bear?" I asked. "They should be worried about the little humans who will be challenging him!"

By the time Victor made his appearance, the fans didn't know what to believe. We offered free tickets and prizes for people who dared wrestle him, but with all the talk about his being trapped and starved no one volunteered. I thought it was funny what a little publicity could do. Hundreds of people had wrestled Victor without injury, but the Anti-Cruelty people insisted that not just anyone from the crowd should get to wrestle the bear. I guess they were afraid someone might try to pull a knife or something. The show had to go on, so I wrestled Victor. To this day people who have forgotten the big crowds and the winning teams will remember me as the fool who dared wrestle a starved bear! Victor politely refrained from falling on me each time he whipped me to the floor, but he not so politely also forgot to use Scope. What breath!

By the end of my first year in Chicago the attendance had risen from a 3000 average to over 10,000. The Bulls made it to the playoffs. I now had confidence that I could run an NBA club, and I had become active at Moody Church and in the FCA and had more speaking engagements than I could handle. At each engagement I was given opportunities to share Christ with basketball fans. I didn't see how things could get better or more exciting.

The 1970–1971 season was a sign of good things in the Bulls' future. For the first time, Chicago had a winning record. Dick Motta led the club to fifty-one victories in eighty-two games and we edged out the Phoenix Suns for a playoff berth. The Los Angeles Lakers beat us in the first round in seven games, and that was a foretaste of our fate. For the next two years Chicago would make it to the playoffs on the wings of fifty-plus victories—only to be eliminated by the Lakers.

Motta was named Coach of the Year by his colleagues, and I was really proud of him. Dick is a single-minded man, totally obsessed with basketball. He speaks directly and pulls no punches. His voice has been described as a piercing monotone. I found him totally enjoyable and invigorating to be with, and we spent hours together. I would have done anything for the man, and I often found myself explaining away his rash statements or actions. I thought we had an exceptional relationship in spite of an occasional difference of opinion. Hassles that arose later would prove me wrong.

The Bulls really came into their own during the 1971–1972 NBA season. Everything seemed to be clicking on the floor as they charged to fifty-seven victories, only to finish second to the unstoppable Milwaukee Bucks. Injuries caught up with them by playoff time, and the Lakers blew out in four straight games. It was humiliating after such an outstanding regular season showing. For me, however, the season was a personal highlight. Promotions were working like magic and I really felt that I was growing as a Christian.

In the spring of 1971 I began working with some of the committees arranging the summer Chicago Crusade of Billy Graham. I was happy to be helping out with publicity and advice, but I was floored when they asked if they could schedule me to tell my own story during one of the meetings. I could hardly believe that God would allow me such an opportunity. I prayed long and often during the days before the June meetings. I wanted the Spirit of God to speak through me.

When the night finally came I was surprisingly calm. McCormick Place was jammed with 40,000 people and the entire service went just as I had imagined it would. Ethel Waters sang. Cliff Barrows was the host. I was in awe of the event, but I was ready. When I stood to speak I felt as if God were speaking through me. I just tried to communicate the thrill I experienced when Christ came into my life and forgave my sins. I told of my peace of mind and joy. And I shared the story of how, when I had turned my self-centeredness over to God, he had changed me and had taken over calling the shots in my career.

The evening was a thrill I'll never forget. It comes back to me now and then as clearly as if it were yesterday.

What a privilege to share with such a large audience what Christ had done for me! I did not know that a beautiful young girl was watching me from her seat in the choir. Jill Marie Paige had seen me at some ballgames and had read about me somewhere. She listened with interest to my story that night and decided that she would like to meet me. She never got close in the crowds that night. But she wasn't about to give up. Nearly six months later, when she read that I was scheduled to speak at a special Thanksgiving service at Moody Church, she told her mother that she was going to go and meet me. She had been zeroing in on that night for weeks. She and her family were visiting in Wheaton on Thanksgiving Day, so Jill broke away early and drove down to Moody Church alone.

I was sitting in the front row signing autographs for some kids after the service when Jill walked up. I stood. "Would you mind signing my program for my third-grade class?" she asked.

This young schoolteacher was really striking. She had deep dark eyes and long brown hair. Her smile was bright and her teeth were perfect. "Sure," I said. "And you sign mine. And while you're at it, put your phone number by your name."

Of course, I was totally unaware that this meeting had been planned. Jill had been talking about it with her mother and grandmother for some time. She floated home from the church that night, mission accomplished. With hardly an effort on her part, I had shown immediate interest. I thought *I* was in command, but her whole family was praying about this relationship!

A little over a week later I called Jill. She wasn't home. Her mother left a message for her with my number on it. All the message said was "Guess who called?" When Jill got back to me she apologized for being tied up that weekend with the Bill Gothard Seminar in Chicago.

That impressed me—but it still hurt to be turned down. I probably wouldn't have called again if Jill hadn't kept in touch. But she did. She sent me a Christmas card with a little good luck note in it. And I received another greeting from her around New Year's. A few days later, on a Wednesday, I called her. (I found later that she was just sick thinking that she had lost me by turning me down that first time. Her persistent conniving and plotting flattered me to no end when I learned of it several months later. I was completely oblivious to it at the time.)

I read in a Dale Carnegie book that the way to secure an answer is to give a person a choice. "I'd like to see you this weekend," I told her. "What's better for you: Friday or Saturday?" She chose Friday, but it didn't turn out to be much of a date.

We had a game that night, so I left a ticket for her. After the game I took her out to dinner. Jill was shy and scared. We had lost the game, so I was down. It had been a long day. It was an O.K. evening, but I was not excited. Jill could tell, I learned later, and she was worried. Her mother kept praying and telling her, "Jill, have faith."

In late January 1972 the Bulls played a Sunday afternoon game. After the game I was to speak at an FCA meeting at a church in Evanston. On the way out of the stadium I saw Jill waiting at the gate. "What are you doing here?" I asked.

"I just wanted to say hi," she said, smiling. *Not a bad move,* I conceded. I invited her to go to the church with me, more out of a feeling that she deserved it than that I really wanted her to come. I thought she had really played it well and I was beginning to see that she was unashamed to show an interest in me. I liked that, but I still felt nothing serious for her.

I saw her once in February and again in March, and still nothing was happening to me. She was really nice, and very pretty, but somehow I felt that we weren't really communicating. Whenever I talked with her on the phone I felt inhibited. Uncomfortable. We saw each other very infrequently in April, May, June, and July. Then I was gone to a summer camp in New York for several days. I called her when I returned. Suddenly we were able to talk. No games—no fronts. I enjoyed it. I called her the next night, and the next, and the next, and the next. I wouldn't say that I had flipped for her, but I found myself looking forward to talking with her each day. *Something* was happening.

I realized how unobservant I had been when I learned that she had been in several beauty contests. In fact, she had just won the Miss Western Cook County pageant and was thus eligible for the Miss Illinois competition. I thought, *Hey, I may have a live one here.* I saw her a little more and met her family. What a family! They are all musically talented and wonderful people. I was becoming more impressed with this girl every day.

When she entered the week-long Miss Illinois contest I sent her some flowers and a telegram. I saw some of the shows that week and found that she was an accomplished pianist, violinist, and vocalist. I also realized that she was the most beautiful girl I had ever met. She seemed more impressed that I was there to see her than that she herself was competing. That did something to me, too.

On the final night of the pageant I sat with her parents. We were all very nervous when Jill was announced as one of the ten finalists. She was still in the running when they narrowed the field to five, then to just two. Now we weren't so nervous. It was in the bag. Jill was obviously the prettier of the two. I patted Mrs. Paige's hand. "Relax, Ma," I said. "We've got it made." It suddenly hit me. *If Jill is named Miss Illinois I can kiss her goodbye for a year!* Suddenly I found myself half rooting against her. But when she was announced as the runner-up

I couldn't even speak. Many people felt that she should have been the winner. Even Judi Ford of Rockford, a former Miss America, told me that Jill was the prettiest and most talented runner-up she had ever seen.

Jill seemed totally content with the decision. She was happy to have been involved. I could hardly believe how calmly she took it, but it was for real. I was so upset that I didn't say anything for about an hour.

The next morning I was to take her to a breakfast, the final event of the pageant. As I stood before the mirror shaving, Billy Graham's Hour of Decision program was coming from the radio in the other room. I could barely hear George Beverly Shea singing. I couldn't even make out the song, but it was beautiful. One instant I was shaving and the next I just broke down and sobbed. God had, for some reason, chosen that moment to zap me with the discovery of Jill. It was as if He had spoken to my heart, "O.K., big fella, it's over." It was crystal clear: I had found a wife. I hadn't even known I was looking!

Later that day I took Jill to meet Norm Sonju and his wife. I had met Norm at a camp three summers before and we had become best friends. I trusted him and often looked to him for spiritual guidance. We talked with the Sonjus for over an hour. I was looking for some kind of acceptance or approval of Jill on the part of my friends. It was a vain move, but I wanted to be sure that people would agree with my discovery. I determined not to call Norm to ask his opinion. I wanted him to call me.

A few days later he called. He was excited about Jill! It was the last affirmation I needed. I didn't propose to Jill. The way she remembers it, we were just talking in the car and I said, "Well, I guess we'll end up getting married." I bought her a ring and told her that she could go ahead and plan the wedding. The Bulls were in the process of being sold, so I told her that everything would have to be tentative since I didn't know if the team would still be in Chicago or even if I would have a job or not. We decided that if any roadblocks popped up in the planning, we would postpone things awhile.

Anyone who has ever planned a wedding knows that roadblocks appear at almost every turn. But not with Jillo. She had worked too hard and long on nailing me and she wasn't about to let anything hold things up! The next thing I knew we had found a nice big church which was available on the day the Bulls began a week's road trip. Three months after the Miss Illinois Pageant, we were married in the Wheaton Bible Church. I invited all the Bulls fans. We had nearly a thousand guests. Luckily, it rained or we might have had five or six thousand. (Friends still ask if we had a halftime show!)

Jill fitted my spiritual temperature perfectly. I couldn't have coped with a superspiritual gal who could quote the whole Bible to me; I needed someone who was solid in her faith and yet still learning and struggling as I was in the Christian walk. Jill had received Christ as a child. She made her decision at an evangelistic service. The speaker? George Sweeting.

What a pleasure it was to come home to a loving wife every day. I had waited many years to even consider marriage, but Jillo has certainly been worth the wait. Besides loving me, she has proved to be a real sports fan, a great conversationalist, and quite a tease. We laugh a lot and have so much fun that I wonder what I ever did with my time as a bachelor. I'm always proud to be seen with her and frustrated when I have to be away for a few days. Just when I thought that God couldn't get any better, He gave me Jill. I don't know what I would have done without her when the first Chicago storm clouds began to brew. So far my life in Christ had been a piece of cake. Now it would be tested.

9

That Toddlin' Town

Some of the greatest days of my life were spent in Chicago, but I couldn't have stayed. Not with things the way they were.

That may sound strange coming from the guy who received much of the credit for making a success of the fast-dying Chicago franchise, but my Chicago dream had turned into a nightmare. Things had breezed along for more than three years and I had enjoyed success at every turn. You often hear people say that Chicago is a nice place to visit, but. . . . Or they say they'd like to live *near* Chicago but not in the city. That wasn't so with me. I loved Chicago.

There was never a dull moment in the capital of the Midwest. I had married a Chicago girl and we had begun our married life in Chicago. I thought it was the greatest city in the world in which to live and work. The Bulls were winning, the FCA was booming, Jill and I were being fed at Moody Church, I was working with the best coach in the NBA, and the Bulls had just been sold to new owners. What could go wrong? Everything.

I'd had my share of hassles trying to deal with ballplayers and their agents. No one is really happy unless he thinks he has somehow talked himself into more money than he's worth. But at the same time I can see a player's point in asking for big money. If we don't pay, there's another league that will. We can't afford to lose good players to the ABA. And players are pros only for a limited number of years. They have to make their money while they're playing because they'll never make the same kind of money again. I try to be fair and honest with them.

I thought I was being fair to Bob Love. Bob is a great forward and was a tremendous asset to the Bulls. He led the team in scoring and was considered a superstar by many experts—including himself. I thought we should pay him what he was worth. He was making $22,000 when he came to the Bulls in 1969. Six weeks into the season I tore up his contract and raised him $5000. The new contract called for another raise of the same amount the following year.

Bob was playing such brilliant basketball that in the spring of 1971 we decided to start again from scratch. I worked up a five-year pact with Bob and his lawyer which worked out to almost $150,000 a year including deferred payments and benefits. I felt that we had made a good deal.

Dick Motta had always told me that he did not want to have anything to do with the money end of player negotiations. He kept me posted on who he thought was valuable and deserved better money, and I kept the exact figures from him at his request.

In the summer of 1972, when the club was in the process of being sold, I had promised Love that we would renegotiate his contract yet another time. He had a new agent who had convinced him that he was worth superstar money. We were already paying him well, but he had overextended himself and had some pressing debts. I reviewed his contract and his playing record and promised him that we would work something out. I thought the most equitable sólution for Bob and the ballclub would be to have us help pay off some of his obligations. He agreed. Things were slowed, however, by the change in ownership.

Bob got antsy. I was working with his lawyer and we were close to working out a good arrangement for Bob. The team was playing some exhibition games in Hawaii. Thousands of miles from home, frustrated and upset, Bob blasted me to the sportswriters. The story broke in Chicago that I was dragging my feet and that I hadn't fulfilled my promises to Bob. Meanwhile his playing suffered because he was apparently taking his off-court problems onto the floor with him. Motta blew up. He asked Bob what was wrong.

Bob told him that I had lied. He said he wasn't playing well because he wasn't happy. Motta will not forgive that in a ballplayer, and I agree that it is terribly bush to let personal problems affect the team.

When the Bulls returned, Dick wanted to take over the negotiations with Love. "Just let me handle it," Dick said. "I'll tell him to fulfill his present contract or sit on the bench. Not another team in the NBA will touch him." Dick was right about that. Bob was obviously not happy, so we tried trading him. We didn't get a single bite.

"Let me handle it," Motta insisted. "He blasted you in the papers, so let him just take his contract the way it is."

"I can't do that, Dick," I said. "I made a promise to this kid that we'd work out a deal for him. We're close to finalizing a deal, so I'll handle it."

I had incensed Dick and I knew it. We renegotiated Love's contract and Bob was happy—at least for the time being. (The next fall, Love would return with yet another agent and try again. Dick would get to deal with him alone on that one; I was watching from Atlanta.)

Things became cool between Motta and me. We had

been close and it was disappointing to see him let the Bob Love fiasco come between us. We had battled together and we had seen the Chicago Bulls become a contender for the NBA championship. But now, I felt, he was not treating me as a friend and colleague. He was distant and curt. Then I gave a sizable raise to Clifford Ray, our second-year center. We had signed Cliff for very little money. With bonuses for making good and fringe benefits, his salary for the first year worked out to about $42,000. That isn't bad for a rookie, but he deserved much more, and we had promised that he would get it.

His agent was asking for a four-year deal at $500,000. It was steep, but Cliff was easily worth $100,000 a year. In a few years he could be worth twice that. If we agreed to the four-year pact, we would be paying through the nose for the first two years, but the last two might be real bargains. Besides, our other center, Tom Boerwinkle, had undergone knee surgery. If he went down in a heap early in the season, Ray would be able to name his own salary. I gambled and signed Ray for the half-million deal.

Motta heard the figures and the fire was refueled. Dick claimed that paying a second-year center that kind of money would make the kid think he's a superstar. The record proves that I had made the right decision. Two weeks into training camp Tom Boerwinkle reinjured his knee. He was out for the season, but we were O.K. We had Ray locked in for four years. We were paying him well, granted, but he played well too. With him at center the team has never won less than fifty games in a season.

Lester Crown, the leader of the new owners, had made me feel secure. He told me on two occasions that the main reason he had bought into the franchise was because Dick and I were there. "The day you leave," he said, "is the day I sell."

"Lester, that is the highest compliment you could pay

a man," I said. I was continuing with the promotional gimmicks, and the attendance figures kept rising. But things weren't right with Dick. He was shopping for a new job with three other teams. The sportswriters predicted his departure all winter, right up to playoff time. Then the lid blew off.

Milwaukee and Los Angeles wound up the season with identical records. The Bulls were to play the club with the best record, so L.A. and Milwaukee were scheduled to meet in a one-game championship. The Lakers balked. Their players said that their contracts called for just eighty-two regular season games. They weren't about to play another game before the playoffs.

On Thursday before the first weekend of the playoffs, the league held a special coin toss to see who would play the Bulls. Had the toss gone in favor of Milwaukee, the Bulls would have made the short trip north for a ballgame the following evening. But the toss went to the Lakers. The commissioner's office called to tell me that we were to play L.A. the next night. "You can't expect our ballclub to play on the West Coast with one day's notice," I said. "There must be time allowed for traveling and settling in and practicing. The Lakers have the home court advantage already. The Bulls will be in no shape to play tomorrow night." I was told that we had no choice—unless we chose to forfeit the game. I called Dick.

There was a moment of silence after I broke the news. I could feel his anger rising even before he spoke. "There's no way!" he said. "I'm getting tired of us getting kicked around all the time. We can't play in L.A. tomorrow night. Why didn't you refuse?"

"I had no choice, Dick," I said. "It's play or forfeit."

"Don't you ever get tired of being pushed around?" he said. I tried to cool him down, but it was no use. I wished him luck.

In Los Angeles the next night Ben Bentley tried to

keep Dick from the press. No go. Dick told the writers that the Chicago management was spineless, that we hadn't backed him in his opposition to the decision. The Bulls lost that game but took the Lakers to seven games before being eliminated. We led with seconds remaining in the final game when the Lakers rallied to stop us before a national television audience. It was a terrible, bitter defeat.

I was called into Lester Crown's office the first Friday in May 1973. "What would you think of the idea of giving up player negotiations so you could concentrate on your promotional specialities?"

I raised my eyebrows.

"Wouldn't it be a good idea to have Dick handle player negotiations since he's so close to the playing situation?" he continued.

"No, I don't think so," I said. His suggestion rocked me. "I think the worst thing for a ballplayer would be to have to go out and play for the guy he haggled with about his salary. Anyway, the job shouldn't be left in the hands of one person. Everyone needs more input, a check-and-balance system." Dick and I had always worked together that way.

Lester Crown thanked me for my opinions. A month later I was asked to announce that Dick Motta was taking over the duties of director of player personnel. I was to remain in charge of promotion, public relations, and ticket sales.

I made the announcement with no comment. I was so bitterly crushed that I couldn't sort out my emotions. I didn't know what hurt me most. The demotion? The loss of my most important responsibility? I was bewildered, confused, dazed.

Writers asked me daily how I felt about the change. I was in too much of an emotional upheaval to be able to comment without bitterness. Jill and I prayed daily that I would get victory from Christ over the hatred and contempt I felt. I would not answer the writers until I had it all sorted out. I did not want to go off half-cocked.

I didn't get victory over my feelings until several days later. I had spent hours wondering, talking with Jill and some friends, and praying. I saw no reason for such a shakeup in my life. It would have been easy to demand that God make everything the way it was before. But who was I to deserve a bed of roses? I just trusted God's word, which says, In *everything* give thanks because *all* things are working together for good. The sportswriters asked how long I would be happy as a ticket salesman. "Not long," I admitted frankly.

Perhaps here was where the hand of God came in. Something had to get me out of Chicago. I could have coped with the situation, but Arthur Wirtz, one of the new owners, was asserting himself more and more as the year went on. He was to take over all decision-making and things would be run his way or not at all.

Wirtz is a multimillionaire. And he's strictly business—no hobbies. He works all day long. Well into his seventies, Mr. Wirtz is six-foot-six and weighs 300 pounds. He's an intimidating figure. He never thought too much of my promotional philosophy. All the halftime hoopla was just so much baloney to him.

When he took over, he insisted that everyone in the stadium pay the full price. And the price was far higher than it had ever been. The fan was no longer treated as a guest. He was treated as a necessity. (Attendance dropped, though Chicago had the best season of its history last year.)

I believe that God knew that I would not be comfortable in that hard-nosed business atmosphere, even if I had kept my player salary responsibilities. I had promised the Bulls total loyalty for as long as I would be there. But less than twenty-four hours after the stories circulated that I had been deposed, undercut, knifed, or whatever word

the writers were using that day, I received a call from
Tom Cousins, president of the Omni group, which owns
the hockey and basketball teams in Atlanta. I had known
Tom when he was the principal owner of the Hawks for a
few years before joining the Omni people. He was a
Christian and a friend of Leighton Ford.

"With your new situation in Chicago," he said, "would
you be interested in talking with us down here?" I would
have stayed in Chicago for another year if God had led me
that way, because I needed a platform from which to share
Christ. But here was an opportunity to leave a bad situation. It was a blessing from God. I couldn't think of a
bigger challenge or a better city to move to than Atlanta.

I made a very quick decision after meeting with the
Omni group. Once again God had taken care of my career
for me. The time was right for moving on. I would have a
few weeks to prepare for the opening of the basketball
season in Atlanta, and I was excited. To coin Ben Bentley's
own phrase, things in Chicago had become like amateur
night in Dixie. So I was glad to be leaving. Leaving for
Dixie. And it wouldn't be amateur night there. Not if God
and I could help it.

10

The Ultimate Victory

Leaving Chicago was hard after four years with the Bulls, but a new city is always exciting. And this time, after four similar moves, I didn't come alone. I brought my most exciting Chicago friend with me: my wife Jill.

Her folks helped with last-minute arrangements and saw us off. It was a tearful goodbye (mine always are), but once on the road we could hardly wait to get here. We had a lot of our stuff shipped in a moving van, but we'd heard scary stories of damaged belongings, so we packed the china and glassware and other valuables in a rental truck and drove it ourselves. We wanted to be sure to have a place to sleep without waiting for the movers too, so we packed our mattress. We regretted that.

What a time we had getting here! Besides the usual trouble finding a motel and parking the cumbersome truck, we had some laughs. Jill drove part of the way. That was a laugh for me—not because she didn't do well, but because she simply doesn't look the part.

Having her along soon proved valuable. When the outside rearview mirror blew off the truck a few hours north of Atlanta, Jill came up with an ingenious idea. Whenever

I wanted to pass, I held her compact mirror out the window to check traffic. How did I ever get along without her? In less than two months we'll have been married a year. I was thirty-one when I met her. I'd waited several years for just the right girl. She was worth the wait.

Jill took care of the thousand and one details that accompany moving to a new city. I would have been lost trying to acquaint myself with the Hawks, the Omni, setting up my office, and all the rest. She found us a beautiful, three-bedroom apartment and began making it our home. We realized immediately that we should have trucked the mattress flat rather than on its side, or at least we should have let someone pack it who knew what he was doing. During the long haul to Atlanta, the insides of the mattress had shifted. It was a complete, lumpy wreck. Until we bought a new one, we spent a few nights on the floor in a sea of blankets and towels.

Our early days in Atlanta were really exciting. The Southern hospitality brought back memories of Spartanburg. I threw myself into lining up promotions, getting player negotiations under way, and just getting acquainted with the new surroundings. Jill and I saw several of Hank Aaron's last homeruns as he ran his lifetime total to 713 by the end of the 1973 season.

I accepted many speaking engagements to all kinds of civic clubs and community organizations. I wanted to do anything necessary to expose Atlanta to the Hawks. And I was also able to share my faith often at these gatherings. The speaking I enjoyed most was sharing with the pregame chapel services of the visiting baseball teams who were in town to play the Braves.

Some baseball managers hold their chapel services on a semiformal invitation basis. If the players want to go, they go, and if they don't, they don't. Sparky Anderson of the Cincinnati Reds handles his differently. Before a doubleheader I met with him and a few players. Then he closed the clubhouse doors and called everybody together. Everybody. No volunteers. No invitations. Just everybody sitting in front of their lockers. Sparky introduced me and gave me ten minutes. In his introduction, Sparky told the players of his meeting Jill at the all-star game in Kansas City. He told them he thought she was the prettiest lady he had ever seen.

I spoke briefly to the Reds about love. Friendly love, family love, and the unconditional love of God. "I challenge you," I concluded, "with the adventure and excitement of inviting Christ into your life. In my opinion, when Christ is in your life and you're playing for God, you're going to be a better ballplayer. Your past is forgiven; your future is sealed. All you need worry about is today. Doing your best—your best for God."

Afterward I got Johnny Bench to sign a baseball for Jill. He wrote "To Jill, Love ya, Johnny Bench." Then I went to the Braves' dressing room and got a pretty fair hitter to write, "Best Wishes, Henry Aaron" on it. We've got it at home in a plastic case above the fireplace, so that ought to keep Jill for a while.

I spoke at the chapel service of the Houston Astros before the last game of the regular season in Atlanta. Jerry Reuss, who had served up Hank Aaron's seven-hundred-thirteenth homerun pitch the night before, was there along with outfielder Bob Watson, coach Bob Lillis, pitcher Ken Forsch (who had arranged the meeting), and Dave Roberts, the left-hander who had the ominous task of facing Hank Aaron on the last day of the baseball season.

I spoke briefly on Mao Tse-tung's four absolutes, which Mao feels are essential in taking over the world for communism. We'd do well to apply the absolutes of this atheist to our Christian faith: absolute acceptance, absolute dedication, absolute discipline, and absolute action. Maybe if we were as serious about Jesus as they are about their ideologies, there would be more Christians than communists in the world.

Forsch and Roberts invited Jill and me for coffee after the chapel service. It was thrilling to spend an hour or so with the man who would have the eyes of the sports world upon him all afternoon as he tried to keep from getting into the record book with Henry Aaron. His teammates kidded him that, if he let Henry hit the record-tying homer, he'd be named to the Hall of Shame. We found Dave very relaxed. He's new in his faith and seems very enthusiastic and dedicated.

We had to wait in line for tickets to the game. Finally, a decent baseball crowd in Atlanta: over 40,000. We sat through a steady drizzle. It was a strange feeling to see a man pitch after having spent the morning with him. We had to wait a year to see Henry Aaron break the homerun record.

Living every day in love for two years has been worth more to me than the other thirty-plus years of my life. I'm not sure how I could have coped with the Chicago situation alone. To have Jill there made even the darkest moments of turmoil and confusion bearable. Because no matter what happened I would still have Jill. She would look forward to my coming home. She would listen. She would pray. She would counsel. She would love me.

When the private line rang in my Atlanta office at around noon one fall day in 1973, I was sure it was Jill. Few others know that number. She was laughing and crying at the same time and she could hardly speak. "Happy anniversary, Daddy," she finally blurted out. I felt as if my blood had stopped flowing.

"Jill, really?"

She was still crying. "Dr. Harrison told me I'd better get out my knitting needles," she said. I laughed and she cried. We had prayed for months about starting a family. With the state of society in our country and the world, it's no small decision to bring a new life into being. We didn't know what the state of the economy or even the presidency would be when our child would be born. We didn't know if the baby would grow up in freedom or chaos.

By the time the baby was to be born in June of 1974, Jill and I would have enjoyed our last months together alone. Later there would be trips that Jill could no longer take with me. She wouldn't be able to come to all the home games. We wouldn't be free to pick up and go to Disney World in Orlando as we had done that anniversary weekend. We, and especially Jill, would be more tied down— and strangely, we knew we would love it.

For the 1973–1974 season we needed something to look forward to. When I started feeling sorry for myself because of the fate of the Hawks, I knew I could still look ahead to June. The Bulls, during my four years in Chicago, had never lost more than three straight games. The first time the Hawks lost four in a row I was really depressed. The team had showed so much promise from the beginning that it was a terrible disappointment when things took a turn for the worse.

The team had started impressively, even leading the division for several days early in the season. The Hawks had made the postseason playoffs every year for more than a decade, and it seemed like a sure thing again. But then the troubles began. With a team of such varied individual stars, Cotton had trouble getting the Hawks to play well as a team. It wasn't that anyone was really selfish, but somehow the club simply wasn't cohesive. They couldn't win the big games. Every once in a while they would upset a Chicago or a Milwaukee, but the lesser teams were giving us fits.

I had hope that by televising several of our road games we would boost our home attendance. The fans would see hot-shooting Lou Hudson and flashy Pete Maravich lead the Hawks to a tough win and then would fill the stadium the next time we had a home game. But it didn't happen that way. The first seventeen road games after New Year's netted us sixteen losses. At that point we had televised twenty-four season games, winning just four and losing nineteen of the others by lopsided scores. It was a nightmare.

Near the end of the season the NBA approved the entry into the league of New Orleans, an expansion club. Fred Rosenfeld, a Los Angeles lawyer, was president of the group of new owners, and I called to congratulate him in March.

We chatted awhile. Then Rosenfeld said, "We sure want to talk to you about Pete Maravich."

I laughed it off. Rumors had flown for months about how New Orleans would make a bid for our superstar. Pete is from Louisiana, and his name is magic there. The most strategic move the new club could make would be to get an established hometown star to build the gate during the difficult growing years. But the new team didn't have anyone to trade for Maravich. "You couldn't give us enough," I told Rosenfeld.

A month or so later the season was over. I had kept in touch with Rosenfeld, though I doubted we could ever really get together on the Maravich deal. It was no secret that we wanted to trade Peter. He's a good kid and a great player, but it takes more than great players to make winning teams. We hadn't made the playoffs and had not been impressive, so we were anxious to make a trade, even to the point of dealing Pistol Pete. But we weren't about to give him away. We wanted two established front-line ballplayers, and we weren't getting that kind of offer from anyone in the NBA.

It became obvious that the New Orleans people really wanted Pete. But they had no players. Before the college draft they would choose one player each from the rest of the teams in the league, but each team had the right to protect its seven top players from the expansion draft. The best New Orleans could do would be to get a bunch of eighth men. We wouldn't trade a talent like Maravich for a busload of subs. Rosenfeld wanted to know just what it would take to get Maravich. I started listing. He didn't flinch, and I began to realize that we were on the verge of one of the biggest trades in the history of pro sports. With Cotton in the background telling me what he needed and Rosenfeld on the phone telling me what he could offer, we set the framework for an unbelievable deal.

Finally New Orleans agreed to an offer we couldn't refuse. I'll always believe, along with most basketball experts, that we committed little short of highway robbery, but that is not to put down New Orleans. They couldn't wait to see how their draft picks would pan out. They needed to get Maravich at any cost. And they paid.

First, they gave us the right to draft the first guard and forward in the expansion pool—we got Dean Meminger from New York and Bob Kauffman from Buffalo. Then we get their first-round draft choice in 1974 and 1975, and their second-round choices in 1975 and 1976; and in 1976 and 1977 we get to use either their first choices or ours, whichever are most advantageous to us. In effect, we are getting eight top draftees who could, in four or five years, be worth an entire franchise. The New Orleans club is bound to finish low in the standings the first few years. That means their draft choices, which are now ours, will be among the first each year.

Cotton Fitzsimmons and I approached John Wilcox, president of the Omni group, and told him we wanted to make the trade. He approved, and Rosenfeld flew in to sign the agreement. Then there was the matter of talking Pete into the deal. He has a no-trade contract, which means he had to approve the deal.

I visited Maravich at his apartment, which is a huge place with several bedrooms. You'd think Pete has a maid, but he does his own cooking and housekeeping, and his home is just immaculate. "I'll come right to the point,

Pete," I said. "We've been made a fantastic offer for you. We feel it's a trade we have to make." I told him why I thought the trade would be good for him and the Hawks, and I told him I wanted him to approve it.

"Well," he said quietly, "I'll have to talk with my lawyers." He was shocked. Pete and his lawyers felt that we should have contacted them during the negotiations, but we had no such obligation. Had the deal fallen through, we'd have looked silly and would have offended a player for no reason. They threatened to veto the move and demanded more money from the New Orleans club, but New Orleans was still willing to pay the price. They agreed on a new contract and called me. New Orleans, with Pete there, held a news conference at the same time we did in Atlanta, announcing the deal on May 3, my thirty-fourth birthday.

I was happy. All those draft possibilities could be awesome.

With a beautiful basketball facility and some of the best individual talent in the league, Cotton Fitzsimmons and I wondered daily what we needed to make the team jell. I still enjoyed promoting and providing a good time for the fans. We had a 130-pound pumpkin and a costume contest for Halloween, reduced prices for fans with the biggest feet when Bob (size 22) Lanier of the Pistons was in town, Mighty Mite Nite for the shorties when Little Nate Archibald of the K.C. Omaha Kings was in, Sky High Nite for the tall folks, and we even gave a free ticket to one fan who claimed he had been discriminated against because he was "too average!"

But as the Hawks continued to lose more than they won, there were fewer and fewer fans to entertain. Three things kept me going. First, I'm not a quitter. I know there are a million fates in this world worse than having a problem drawing fans to a pro basketball game. I was healthy, happy, in love, making good money, living comfortably, active in the thriving First Baptist Church, making many new friends, and working at a challenging job.

Second, I was looking forward so eagerly to the birth of our child. What a thrill it was to go with Jill to the doctor's office and hear for myself the tiny rapid heartbeat! Nothing in my job could be more important than my wife and unborn child.

Third, and most important, I looked forward to the return of Jesus Christ. That is the only sure thing I know. Even the birth of our baby was not certain. We couldn't know in advance if our baby would be big or small, a boy or a girl, an athlete or a scholar, an all-night sleeper or a cryer. We could predict nothing except that Jill was due last June. With the return of Christ it is just the opposite. We know everything we need to know except the date and time. And since we don't know, we can look forward to it every day. He may not return in our lifetime, but there's no reason why He couldn't or shouldn't. I used to wonder what could be more exciting than the work I'm in. Now I know: being with the Christ who changed my life and assured me of an eternity with Himself.

I remember one night when I was still with the Bulls. The Chicago radio station was carrying the Bulls game live from Phoenix, but the television station was to show a delayed telecast. I have never been able to listen to my own teams on the radio. It's too nerve-racking. For some reason I feel less helpless if I can *see* what's happening rather than just listening to it.

So I left the radio off and didn't turn on the television until the news was off. I wanted to watch the delayed telecast of the game without knowing the outcome. Early in the second half, the game was very close and I was enjoying the tension. I found myself shouting and carrying on as I do at the home games, though I knew the game was already over and that nothing I did was going to change the outcome. Then my secretary called. She was shouting and cheering, "Pat, we won! We won! The Bulls won!"

I would rather have seen it myself, but a strange thing happened to me as I watched the rest of that delayed telecast. The Bulls would take a five-point lead and I'd think, *Yeah, here's where they blow it wide open and walk away with it.* Then they'd have some problems and Phoenix (then coached by Cotton Fitzsimmons) would rally and go ahead by four or five. I'd wonder, *How will the Bulls overtake them again?* But I sat there calmly. I wasn't worried. I knew the outcome. It was a sure thing. It was more like watching an opera than a noisy pro basketball game.

With a minute and a half to play in the last quarter the Bulls blew a nine-point lead. The Phoenix crowd was in hysterics, stomping and shouting. With three seconds on the clock, the Suns trailed by one point and they had the ball. They called a time out and set up a play. Normally I'd have been bouncing around on the edge of my seat, going crazy and screaming for the Bulls to stop the play— *Don't let them score!* But I knew the Suns weren't going to score. I sat chuckling. "Go ahead and shoot it up, Babe," I shouted at the television. " 'Cause I know it's not going in." The shot went up and bounced out. What a glorious feeling it was to *know* what was going to happen in that ballgame. I have that same feeling about the return of Christ.

Nothing compares with knowing, despite the personality clashes, the economy, the hatred, the bigotry, and the shortages, that the person who loves Christ and has received God's gift of eternal life will be the ultimate winner. We can't lose. We trust in the power of the resurrected Christ. We go through life battling mortal problems and facing hardships and difficulties, yet we know that it will all be insignificant someday.

I've often been asked if I really believe that Christianity is relevant to the world of professional sports. Perhaps the church or the religion or the code of ethics, or whatever a person might think Christianity is all about, does not directly relate to many problems of today. But to

me Christianity is Christ. And He *is* relevant. In many
ways He is meek and mild and sweet because He loves
me. But He is also gutsy, contemporary, radical, and strong,
a Friend I can depend upon in my world of ups and
downs. Whether the Hawks are winning or losing, the fans
are happy or irate, a rookie is being signed or a veteran
released, my Christ remains constant. It moves me to think
that Christ would have suffered and died for me, even if I
were the only person who ever lived. He loves me.

Many people think that the bum on the street, or the
criminal, or the addict, would be the toughest type of person to reach with the love of God. But I tend to think otherwise. People like me, people who think they're all right
and that they are doing God a favor by just being around,
are the ones who just can't see God for what He is. The
derelicts know what they are. They often seek God. God
had to come looking for me, because I sure didn't think
I needed Him.

I was sure that becoming a Christian would mean
giving up everything I enjoyed for a life of sacrifice and
dullsville. I fought and fought against letting go, giving up,
releasing the reins of my life to God. When I finally trusted
Him enough to take a step in His direction, I found
that He cared more for me than I did. And I've never been
the same.

When the hassles arose in Chicago, the old Pat Williams would have told off a few people, smashed the glass
on top of his desk, ranted and raved and sought revenge.
But there was a new Pat Williams. Because of Christ. I had
been changed. It was nothing I had done; I can't take an
ounce of credit for the new me.

And when it became obvious at the end of the 1973–
1974 season that the Hawks were hopelessly out of the
running for a playoff berth, it was disappointing. I don't
know what the old Pat Williams might have done. Blame
the players? The coach? Luck? The fans? Don't get me

wrong—a disappointing season still hurts. God never promised me a breezy life. But now I find myself anxious to get up and get back to work. To work and worry and plan for the next season. I can't dwell upon defeat and disappointment when I know that the ultimate victory will be mine. Because of Christ.

EPILOGUE

Our son was born on the day of the NBA draft, Monday, May 27, at 5:13 P.M. I was with Jill from labor to birth. It was the most overwhelming worship experience I've ever had. An atheist seeing his baby born would be converted in an instant. You can't come out of a delivery room doubting the existence of God. When the doctor said, "We've got a boy here," I just dropped my head and praised the Lord.

We couldn't think of anything more appropriate to name him than James Littlejohn, after my father and my "second father."

That night during the draft I decided to get my son on the right track in his professional sports career. In the tenth round, as execs from the league office and the other clubs listened via a conference-telephone hookup, I announced Atlanta's next choice. "James Williams," I said.

"Is that Fly?" someone cut in, wondering if we had tried to illegally draft Jim "Fly" Williams, a junior at Austin Peay.

"What school?" asked Si Gourdine, assistant to the commissioner.

"Piedmont Hospital, Atlanta," I said. "Nineteen and a half inches tall, seven and a half pounds." There was silence on the line.

"Disallowed," Gourdine said, chuckling.

Me in my first catcher's mitt.

A baseball fanatic at thirteen.

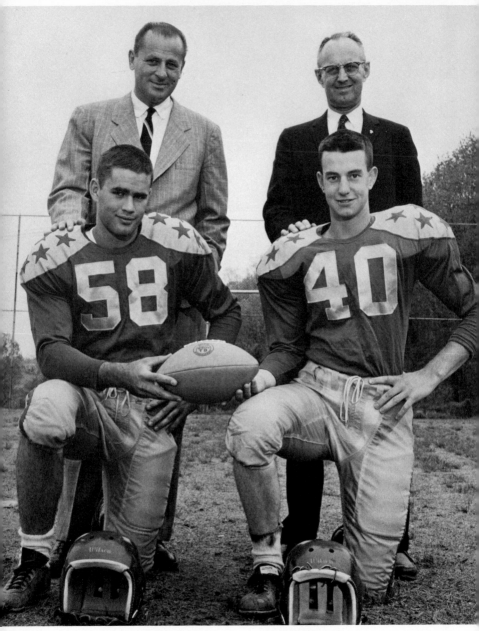

August 1958, fathers and sons—best friend Ruly Carpenter with his dad and here I am with mine.

Miami News

"Why bother? it's a homerun." With the Miami Marlins, summer, 1962. Chet Trail of the Fort Lauderdale Yankees scores a run.

Jay Spencer, Miami News

A funny thing happened on my way to the front office. Bill Durney and I look over my newly signed Phillies contract as his assistant.

With the great Satchel Paige in Spartanburg, summer, 1965.

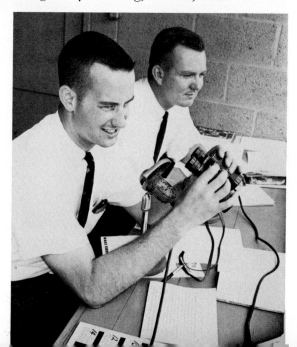

With Bill Veeck at Wake Forest, May 1965.

(opposite) Woody Durham and me—broadcasting Wake Forest foot-ball, fall, 1965.

Here I am giving weight lifter Paul Anderson a lift.

Hammond, Indiana, June 1971—witnessing at a Billy Graham crusade.

Jillo at the Miss Illinois Pageant, August 1972.

Just moved into Atlanta and felt right at home— September 1973.

A zany halftime show at The Omni— "Uncle Heavy and His Porkchop Revue."

(right) Victor, the wrestling bear—just a piece of cake.

Me in my first catcher's mitt.

A baseball fanatic at thirteen.

August 1958, fathers and sons—best friend Ruly Carpenter with his dad and here I am with mine.

Miami News

"Why bother? it's a homerun." With the Miami Marlins, summer, 1962.
Chet Trail of the Fort Lauderdale Yankees scores a run.

Jay Spencer, Miami News

A funny thing happened on my way to the front
office. Bill Durney and I look over my newly
signed Phillies contract as his assistant.

With the great Satchel Paige in Spartanburg, summer, 1965.

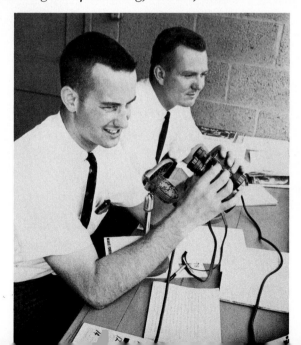

With Bill Veeck at Wake Forest, May 1965.

(opposite) Woody Durham and me—broadcasting Wake Forest foot-ball, fall, 1965.

Here I am giving weight lifter Paul Anderson a lift.

Hammond, Indiana, June 1971—witnessing at a Billy Graham crusade.

Jillo at the Miss Illinois Pageant, August 1972.

Just moved into Atlanta and felt right at home— September 1973.

A zany halftime show at The Omni— "Uncle Heavy and His Porkchop Revue."

(right) Victor, the wrestling bear—just a piece of cake.